D1196720

MSU
LIBRARIES

RETURNING MATERIALS:
Place in book drop to
remove this checkout from
your record. FINES will
be charged if book is
returned after the date

John Wheatley

LIVES of the LEFT is a new series of original biographies of leading figures in the European and North American socialist and labour movements. Short, lively and accessible, they will be welcomed by students of history and politics and by anyone interested in the development of the Left.   *general editor* David Howell

John Wheatley

Ian S. Wood

Manchester University Press

Manchester and New York

Distributed exclusively in the USA and Canada by St. Martin's Press, New York

Copyright © Ian S. Wood 1990

Published by Manchester University Press,
Oxford Road, Manchester, M13 9PL, UK
and Room 400, 175 Fifth Avenue, New York, NY 10010, USA

Distributed exclusively in the USA and Canada
by St. Martin's Press, Inc., 175 Fifth Avenue, New York, NY 10010, USA

British Library cataloguing in publication data
Wood, Ian S.
John Wheatley. — (Lives of the left)
1. Great Britain. Politics. Wheatley John, 1869–1930
I. Title   II. Series
941.082'092'4

Library of Congress cataloging in publication data
Wood, Ian S.
John Wheatley / Ian S. Wood.
    p.   cm. — (Lives of the left)
Includes bibliographical references.
ISBN 0 7190 1994 X
1. Wheatley, John, 1873-1930. 2. Legislators—Great Britain—Biography.
3. Great Britain. Parliament. House of Commons—Biography.
4. Great Britain—Politics and government—1910-1936.
5. Labour Party (Great Britain)—History—20th century.
6. Socialism—Great Britain—History—20th century.
I. Title.   II. Series.
DA574.W48W66 1989
941.082'092—dc20   89-12696
[B]

ISBN 0 7190 1994 X hardback

Set in Perpetua
by Koinonia Ltd, Manchester
Printed in Great Britain
by Robert Hartnoll

Contents

Acknowledgements

I am most grateful to the Carnegie Trust for Scotland and to the Scottish Arts council for the grants which they contributed to the preparation of this book. I am also grateful to all the staff who have helped me in the National Library of Scotland; the Mitchell Library, Glasgow; the libraries of the universities of Edinburgh and Glasgow; Glasgow City Archives; Baillieston Public Library; the Public Record Office at Kew, Surrey; the Passfield Library of the London School of Politics and Economics; the Marx Memorial Library at Clerkenwell Green, London; and the John Rylands Library, Manchester.

I have also been greatly helped by the late Lord Wheatley and his widow Lady Wheatley, the late Lord Fenner Brockway, and the late John Wheatley and Harry McShane. Others whose recollections I have drawn upon include William Weir Gilmour, Mrs Rose Viola and Mrs Jean Huggins. Many others have given me help, encouragement and cheerful company which have contributed towards whatever the end product may be worth. These include Ian Budge, who gave me my chance to re-enter the academic world after a period away from it, John Brown, Henry Cowper, Ian Donmachie, Gerry Douds, Tom Gallagher, Ian MacDougall, David Lindsay, my head of department at Napier Polytechnic, and many more.

Brenda Molony has been an unfailingly patient typist, performing marvels with an at times chaotic script. Manchester University Press have been a pleasure to work with, and I must thank the editor of this series, David Howell, and Sally McCann, the copy-editor, for the indispensable help they have given me. Responsibility for this book's shortcomings remain mine alone but any merits it may have owe much to their good advice.

Finally, my wife Helen has lived under the same roof with the subject of this book for longer than I ever thought she would have to. Without her encouragement, I might not have started or finished it, so I dedicate it to her and to my sons Ben, David and Robbie.

Ian S. Wood

1 Early life

Historical writing on the labour movement has not ignored John Wheatley, (for his voice was an important one in some major debates about the political future of the Irish community in Scotland, and in Britain about Catholicism and socialism, about Labour housing policy and about Labour attitudes to the First World War. He was close, personally and politically, to many of those who shaped the legend, if that is what it was, of the Red Clyde, and was one of the few successes in the 1924 Labour government.

The experience of office without power was decisive for him and he vowed not to repeat it, devoting much of his remaining years to increasingly trenchant and wide-ranging criticisms of what seemed to him the Labour leadership's infirmity of any clear socialist purpose. His career on the British political stage was a brief one, for he sat in Parliament for only eight years before his death in 1930. This may be one reason why, until recently, he lacked a biographer; another may be the absence of any personal papers or correspondence left by him; and a third may be that he never had the charismatic qualities of a Maxton or a MacLean.

This book will seek to piece together the main events of a remarkable life, one given over from early on, against heavy odds, to political thought and action based upon it in the Catholic Irish community in which he grew up, then on behalf of the working class as a whole in Scotland and Britain. Interwoven with this will be an examination of the religious and political ideas which led him to the distinctive place he created for himself in the labour movement in the early decades of this century.

The great Irish migration to Scotland was past its peak when John Wheatley's parents made their decision, in 1876, to leave County Waterford. Little is known of them except that Thomas Wheatley was a labourer who had muscle to sell in the Lanarkshire coalfield where he settled with his family. Braehead, or Bargeddie as it later became known, was one pit village among many on the fringe of the town of Baillieston, and it was there that Thomas Wheatley and his wife set up a home for a family which grew to eight. John Wheatley was their oldest child, having been born in 1869, and followed his father down the pit as soon as he was old enough, probably in 1881 when he was twelve years old.

He found an Irish labour force established in the Scottish coal industry from the middle years of the century, most conspicuously in Ayrshire and Lanarkshire, though there was subsequent movement eastwards by many of the first Irish incomers and their families which affected the whole social geography of large areas of Fife and the Lothians. In Lanarkshire the major coal companies tried to use the immigrant Irish as a lever to control overall wage levels, notably those in the Coatbridge area who wanted cheap coal primarily to feed the area's great iron foundries. Sometimes company agents recruited labour at an agreed price direct from Ireland rather than on a casual basis among the immigrants once they arrived.

The vulnerability of Irish miners to company exploitation affected the whole pattern of unionisation among the labour force as a whole, superimposed as it was upon sectarian conflicts which the Irish immigration brought with it. The story of West—Central Scotland in the middle years of the nineteenth century is one of recurrent, and sometimes violent, tensions brought about by Protestant Irish immigrants and native-born Scots joining forces in Orange Lodges as a counter-weight to the way many Catholics maintained not merely their faith but their political allegiance to Irish Home Rule. Rioting, especially at the time of Orange walks in July, could become serious, while segregated living in identifiable areas and close intermarriage within each community opened fissures of long-term social importance which acted as a brake upon trade union organisation. But by the late 1860s the Irish were beginning to make a visible contribution to the fight for better wages and conditions.

Baillieston itself lay at the western fringe of the Lanarkshire coalfield's expansion, a process greatly assisted by the railway development in the 1870s, and over a dozen pits are known to have been worked in the area; seams and workings extended to well within what are now the city boundaries of Glasgow. The last pit of this once flourishing coalfield was the Cardowan pit at Stepps, closed in 1982 after a serious fire. Most of the Baillieston pits had narrow, and often very wet seams, though sufficiently free of gas for naked lights to be used. Mechanised cutting was slow to reach the area and the local pits seem to have been under-capitalised, perhaps because of the keen competition among the companies which worked them, though ultimately the Glasgow Iron and Steel Company and United Collieries achieved a controlling interest in most. The ever-present reality of death and mutilation by roof and rock falls and other causes made Baillieston miners as superstitious as many other pit communities. Those who knew the area recalled a miner's inherited fear of meeting a woman on the way to a shift, something which could make some men forfeit a day's pay rather than tempt fate by going to work. A new recruit would never descend in the same cage as members of his own family, only with men who were strangers to him. When death came it was attended with few formalities. A body, if it could be retrieved, would simply be brought to the top, loaded on a cart and returned to the man's home for washing and laying out. The rattle of the cart's approach during a shift cast a chill of fear over the miners' rows in Baillieston and the sur-rounding villages.

The bleak poverty of life in the Scottish coalfields is well and vividly documented, and Baillieston still appalled an older John Wheatley years later when he found himself back as a speaker. He shared his childhood with seven brothers and sisters, and sometimes a lodger, in a house consisting of a single room, barely 18 feet square, where cooking, dining, mending, studying, sleeping, birth and death all had to take place. For miners' wives life must have been unending toil to organise and feed families in such conditions, without a water supply or lavatory. Sanitation consisted of ash-pit closets 40–50 yards away serving anything up to a dozen families, while fresh water had to be carried in all weathers from 100 yards away. Children often went bare-footed, and the only collars worn in Wheatley's school class were of washable rubber. Illiteracy was the norm among the older generation, and those who could read were often visited by neighbours anxious to hear what was in such newspapers as were on offer locally.

Baillieston's population of some 1,000 was substantially Catholic: some accounts of the area at the turn of the nineteenth century suggest as much as a three-to-one Catholic predominance over Protestants, but the two communities appear to have co-existed, in the main, without overt friction. Church of Scotland representatives attended the opening of the first Catholic parish church in 1894, and accounts of life in Baillieston from these years point to a good deal of goodwill and co-operation across denominational boundaries. The experience of communities elsewhere in Lanarkshire, however, showed how quickly amity and tolerance could evaporate when sectarian allegiances were openly proclaimed. In the same year, during a major strike, an Orange Lodge with its flute band attempted to parade in Baillieston. The predominantly Catholic miners were outraged, as much as anything because local Orange Lodges were regarded as bodies who curried favour with the coal companies. The Orange walk got short shrift: the bandsmen were set upon and their drums and flutes seized and later used for a strike rally.

In the initial period of the town's growth, mass was celebrated two or three miles away at Eastmuir and the faithful made their way on foot since there was no other way. The first mass to be celebrated in Baillieston itself was in a converted stable on Christmas Day 1874, and two years later the Catholic church in Scotland ruled that Baillieston should have a priest of its own. Two then followed each other in the space of two years, until 1879, when Fr Peter Terken, a gifted and dedicated Dutch mission priest who became an important influence on Wheatley, arrived in the parish. Father Terken was to remain in Baillieston for thirty-five years, and the present fine parish church of St Bridget remains a visible memorial to him. It was built in large part through his fund-raising efforts, though in this he was always aided by a congregation mostly of miners and their families who idolised him, and its opening in 1894 was a major event.

Everywhere in the parish Father Terken's figure appears to have been an unmistakable one; he was indefatigable in covering it on foot, soon knowing all there was to know about his congregation. He nearly always carried an ebony walking stick, which he was not averse to using to break up fights or to quell disorder when the town's many public houses closed their doors at weekends. To be named by him from the pulpit for defaulting on one's obligations to the church collection or for any other misdemeanour was a major disgrace in a small and still self-sufficient community, despite its apparent proximity to Glasgow.

Father Terken was also instrumental in launching a Young Men's Society and an active branch of the League of the Cross. When the Irish Foresters Benefit and Friendly Society began to recruit a membership in the area, it named its local branch after him in his honour, and he, in turn, often presided over its meetings, as indeed he did over those of the Irish National League. His presence meant much to the children of the parish as did that of a Bavarian curate, Gisbert Hartmann, who later joined him in the parish. In good time for Christmas each year he always had a barrel of biscuits, oranges and apples shipped over from his home, which were distributed to the parish children, and both he and Father Terken were enthusiastic organisers of special Christmas parties and carol services for them. Patrick Dollan, a younger contemporary of Wheatley's who, like him, worked in the local pits before also going on to make an impact as a journalist, councillor and Labour organiser in Scotland, remembered this when writing of his childhood fifty years later: 'Christmas was then a working day like all the others and we were so isolated from the Christian world on 25 December that we began to wonder if Christmas Day had been denied us for some wicked offence we must have committed in the past. Christmas was a black day for the children of the poor in Baillieston.'[1] The priests who helped to change this had little need of any memorial to themselves.

This, then, was the milieu in which John Wheatley grew up, receiving his first Communion from Father Terken, serving as an altar-boy, attending St Bridget's School, and actively involved in the affairs of the parish once the new church was opened. This church-centred and intensely Irish environment which the migrants created for themselves in Scotland has come under the microscope of those who feel that they were prevented by social controls within their own community from living up to what Engels had claimed was their potential for radicalising the native working class. 'The Irish in Scotland emerged as creators of arks of refuge rather than as builders of barricades,'[2] it has been said, and those who broke the mould and diverged from their expected roles could have quite strong pressure applied to them, as Wheatley himself was to find out. Yet his Catholicism was strengthened by the very circumstances in which he acquired it, and was something he never broke with despite the bitter disagreements he was to have with some of the clergy.

Early promise revealed in school and recognised by Terken in his own religious instruction classes was irrelevant to a twelve-year-old's career prospects in a locality dominated by the pits. At the age of twelve he was at work underground with his father and was joined later by his brothers, and the memory of his initiation to the nether world of manual coal-cutting and drawing and the twelve years he gave to it was something that never left him. In speeches and in writings he frequently reverted to his experiences as a working miner, to the starkness and ever-present danger, but most often to the filth of wet seams, dust and communal defecation. Perhaps it was his reaction to this that later made him the fastidious dresser, whose neat turn-out was often in striking contrast to the wild looks and famously long hair of James Maxton when they had occasion to share a platform at meetings of the Independent Labour party (ILP). At this distance in time, it is possible still to marvel at what gave a working miner sharing a single-roomed house with ten other people the stamina and resolve to continue with an education abruptly cut off by the pits, and to wonder, too, how he managed to find space and light for the business of reading. For read and study he did, as a follow-up to the evening classes which he attended in Glasgow. These were held under the auspices of the city's Athenaeum, a remarkable institution to attend which meant a round trip on foot of ten miles from Baillieston. The Glasgow Athenaeum had been founded in 1847 by voluntary subscription to sponsor public lectures on a wide range of subjects. A succession of Lord Provosts, MPs and business men gave the institution their backing, and, in 1888, it was able to occupy a spacious new building in St George's Place, where it could fulfil its function of offering instruction on public speaking, economics, law, languages and literature, art, drama and music. Modest fees were charged and, to maximise opportunities for students in full-time employment, classes began at seven o'clock in the morning and continued until ten o'clock at night. The ethos of the Athenaeum and its whole social atmosphere seem to have been steeped in contemporary assumptions about the virtues of self-help and individual enterprise, which was, no doubt, why the city's commercial élite bestowed its benediction upon it. Miners from the Lanarkshire coalfield did not predominate among its enrolled students. For Wheatley, the Athenaeum signalled a way out of the Baillieston pits, though he was never to break faith with the miners as a community.

The first work he appears to have taken on leaving the pits in 1893 was in a local public house; then he joined his younger brother, Patrick, in a grocery business which he had set up at 273 Shettleston Main Street and at 2 Budhill Avenue nearby. Shortly afterwards, Wheatley applied, without success, for a licence to sell beer and spirits at the Budhill shop. If this enterprise was anything like others we know of in the locality or further eastwards in Baillieston itself, it probably sold everything from food and confectionery to explosives, pit-oil and lamp-wicks for miners. Wheatley was taken on by his brother as an assistant for thirty shillings a week. For a time the business prospered and young John McGovern, who years later was to be Wheatley's successor as MP for Shettleston, joined them as a messenger-boy, his brother having already been employed in this initial Wheatley venture. The McGoverns were Catholics too, though this appears to have earned them no special treatment. Indeed the older McGovern later recalled earning all of seven shillings a week for what was sometimes a fourteen-hour day.

The relative success of the business provided security, too, for John Wheatley's marriage which took place in 1886 to Mary Meechan, the daughter of an Irish railway maintenance foreman who worked in the area. Patrick Dollan was an altar-boy at the wedding in St Bridget's church and later recalled a sizeable turn-out at what Baillieston miners called a pay-wedding. This meant simply that guests, instead of bringing presents, bought tickets beforehand to defray the cost of the festivities and to help the couple make essential purchases for their new home.

Marrying into his own community in this way cemented Wheatley's links with it. 'Upwardly mobile' he may have been in terms of success achieved in business and later in politics, but he never forgot the poverty from which he had escaped or forgave the social system which continued throughout his lifetime to inflict it upon many of his own family as well as upon the working class in Scotland and in Britain as a whole. Carefully chosen suits, spectacles which he nearly always wore, and a sometimes considerable girth tempted many cartoonists over the years to ridicule an appearance which, they implied, was at sharp variance with the beliefs he espoused. They need not have bothered, for Wheatley's years in Baillieston as a child, then as a miner, implanted memories which never left him. The generous anger at injustice he acquired then would be a constant point of reference for everything he sought to achieve both in local and national politics.

Wheatley remained in the grocery business with his brother until 1901 when financial difficulties required them to sell their interest in it. The accumulated debts took some time to clear. He then took employment with the *Glasgow Observer*, a weekly newspaper founded in 1885 to serve the needs of the large immigrant and Irish-descended community in the west of Scotland. Under the third of its editors, Charles Diamond, who had originally come from Maghera in Derry, the paper expanded rapidly and, indeed, became the nucleus of a newspaper and periodical publishing combine that at one time brought out forty different titles. Diamond, a considerable figure in Irish Home Rule politics, was MP for North Monaghan between 1882 and 1895, and the paper had been strongly Parnellite until the traumas of the O'Shea divorce case. Its support for the Home Rule cause remained unswerving and it was meticulous in its coverage both of Irish news and immigrant politics, church, cultural and sporting life in Scotland. Wheatley was taken on by Diamond's organisation as a canvasser for advertising copy, and he also managed to find part-time employment as manager of a billiards saloon near Glasgow Cross.

His work as a canvasser for the *Observer* brought him into contact with Mandy M'Gettigan, a colourful Irish character already working for the *Glasgow Examiner*, a paper launched in 1885 which also sought to reach the Catholic Irish community in Scotland. Wheatley and M'Gettigan often pooled their efforts to collect advertising copy, working under the name of Dallard and Gill, sometimes resorting to dubious methods in the recollection of their contemporaries. On one occasion, the several irregularities of a local businessman were used to pressurise him into giving their two papers advertising copy.

Wheatley drew a wage of three pounds a week for his work for the *Observer*, but, in 1908, he and M'Gettigan gambled with the launching of their own printing firm. This they call Hoxton and Walsh, though no one of either name was ever connected with it. Initially they handled shopkeepers' advertising calendars, often incorporating Catholic news, and sometimes devotional items for Catholic households. Wheatley and M'Gettigan converted their business, in 1911, into a limited company with a nominal share capital of two thousand pounds. On their issue, M'Gettigan acquired 940, John Wheatley 740, and his brother-in-law, Patrick Meechan, 250. The business prospered and made easier Wheatley's growing involvement first in Irish nationalist then in Labour politics.

2 Politics and faith

By the time he left the pits, Wheatley had become locally active in the Irish Home Rule movement, a natural political apprenticeship, for his own father had been a founder member of a Baillieston branch of the Irish National League. This branch was named after Michael Davitt, the great Fenian and Land League leader, and appears to have been vigorous and radical in its activities. The League had developed as an outgrowth of an increasingly militant and intransigent Irish Parliamentary party, due in large measure in Scotland to the tireless work of John Ferguson, a Protestant Ulsterman who had settled in Glasgow in 1880. From its formation in 1881, its many local branches, with their fund-raising, electioneering and regular meetings, provided an increasingly effective machine with which Parnell and his lieutenants could mobilise the Irish in Britain. At the level of local council politics, branches were increasingly drawn into co-operation with the labour movement. A Workers' Municipal Election Committee in Glasgow in 1895 invited Irish branches to affiliate, and this co-operation proved important in building up Labour and working-class representation in the government of the city before 1914. Baillieston's branch appears to have survived the traumas which Parnell's fall created, and it was into it that the young John followed his father at a time when the movement over much of Scotland was recovering its momentum.

The year 1898, the centenary of what was then the greatest of all Irish rebellions, was a time of intense activity in

Scotland. Full-time organisers worked hard to revive old branches and to create new ones. Over ninety were claimed to be active in Scotland and some, in response to the rise of a militant language movement in Ireland, were offering Gaelic talks, programmes of song and instruction in the language. Others, like the Port Glasgow Patrick Sarsfield branch, were out to catch members young and reduced their qualifying age for membership to five years. Many new branches were, in fact, constituted as part of the new United Irish League (UIL). Delegates of the old National League agreed at a Dublin convention of 1900 to merge with it to become part of what it was hoped would be a new and stronger Home Rule campaign on either side of the Irish Sea.

Wheatley transferred his membership from the League's Baillieston branch to Shettleston after he and his wife moved there, and he was regular in attendance at the local Daniel O'Connell branch, as its regular reports to the nationalist news columns of the *Glasgow Observer* make clear. He quite often took the chair at meetings before being elected as president of the branch in 1901. Taking the chair meant, on occasions, presiding over meetings devoted almost wholly to celebrations of Irish nationhood, as when he introduced one visiting speaker whose theme was 'Ireland, the fount of western civilization'.[1] If this was ethnocentricity, then John Wheatley was not free of it at this early stage of his life. Indeed, he spoke frequently at the O'Connell branch on themes relating to Irish history. Despite a high-pitched speaking voice, he made himself popular with dramatic readings from Irish national history; in fact, he was a strong advocate of special classes for the children of branch members.

Wheatley's time as president saw the Shettleston branch become the League's fourth-largest in Scotland, with a reputation for efficient organisation of its activities and vigorous fund-raising for the Home Rule cause. It made full use, too, of its right to send delegates to the UIL's annual conventions, and Wheatley, in his last presidential year, had been one of three Shettleston branch delegates at the 1903 Bristol convention. There he had contributed effectively to a debate over organisational matters, putting the case for as many branches as possible building or acquiring their own premises rather than being beholden to the church for meeting facilities.

Over and above all this, Wheatley seems to have thrown himself with apparent enthusiasm into the League's social activity. In July 1901, the Shettleston branch organised 700 people for a railway excursion to Helensburgh on the Clyde. Members and their families were led by the Patrick Sarsfield band to Carntyne station and played onto the train with the rousing strains of the 'Boys of Wexford'. Once arrived at Helensburgh, the band led the party to a public park where traditional Irish dancing figured as part of the entertainments. Some made trips by steamer to Garelochhead, and the day was acclaimed as a great success: 'Happy smiling faces which thronged the train on its return journey told a tale of satisfaction.'[2]

Two years later, Wheatley was chosen to represent the branch, along with two other members, on a special organising committee whose brief was the handling of the centennial commemoration of the execution of a great Irish patriot, Robert Emmett. Nearly all UIL branches in Scotland honoured this anniversary and in Shettleston the local branch combined its efforts with the Irish National Foresters' Friendly Society to run a series of indoor meetings and a special parade. Wheatley acted as one of the parade marshalls, green rosettes were worn by all, period costume by many, and one member took the part of Emmett, riding a specially hired bay horse, while as always at the UIL's outdoor ceremonies, bands played to commemorate the patriot dead.

All this can, of course, be categorised merely as the ghetto rituals of a community committed only to the affirmation of its own identity in a Scotland which wanted the Irish as a labour force, but which distrusted, and in many ways rejected, them for reasons both religious and cultural. Indeed, John Wheatley's lifetime was to coincide with a recognisable growth in anti-Irish prejudice even as the level of actual immigration dwindled from its mid-nineteenth-century peak. The political and cultural nationalism of the UIL was seen by some as an act of self-assertion made easier for the immigrants by the very fact that Scotland itself was a society which, beneath the veneer of Victorian capitalist growth, was confused and uncertain about its own loss of identity within the legislative union with England. As Compton MacKenzie was later to put it, 'the Irish who settled in Scotland settled in a country which seemed to them to have surrendered what they had never surrendered – nationhood. They were not willing to suffer a comparable loss of status, and finding where they penetrated little peculiarly Scottish left except religious intolerance and sectarian hate, they preferred to remain expatriate Irish.'[3]

The young John Wheatley's readiness to immerse himself in the political aspirations of the homeland which poverty and want had compelled his parents to abandon, is the story of the Irish in exile, a people, as C. C. O'Brien put it, with history clinging as inexorably to their backs as the Old Man of the Sea clung to that of Sinbad. Even when he re-thought his political priorities to the point of leaving the League and espousing a non-Marxist but radical socialism, he never forgot his Irish descent. Indeed, it proved to be something which his political enemies would seek to use against him.

Intermittently over the period 1904–5 we can identify Wheatley's continued activity in the Shettleston UIL branch, and it remains a problem to pin-point the exact moment, if there was one, of formal severance of his membership. It has been suggested that, by 1906, he was already a socialist by conviction, since in the general election of that year he had acted as agent for the Labour Representation Committee's candidate in the North-West Lanark constituency. This is not in itself proof that Wheatley had left the UIL, for its local branches all supported the Catholic Labour candidate against a Roseberyite Liberal, Dr C. M. Douglas, of predictably lukewarm views on Irish Home Rule, an issue from which the Liberal leadership had been seeking to distance itself ever since Gladstone's retirement. Indeed, the League had already abandoned its uncritical Liberal allegiance. Five years before, in a 1901 by-election in the North-East Lanark seat, the League's executive had, in fact, endorsed a Labour candidate, Robert Smillie, and Wheatley had used his influence to hold the Shettleston branch in line over this decision. In both cases the League's intervention had failed to produce Labour victory. In fact, in North-East Lanarkshire in 1906, it may well have contributed to the phenomenon of a Unionist gain amidst a Liberal landslide.

In the 1905–6 general election in the constituency, the Labour Representation Committee's Joseph Sullivan had, in any case, strong Irish connections, the press referring to him as Roman Catholic, a member of the Ancient Order of Hibernians and of other Irish organisations. His election address could as well be described as radical Liberal as by any other label, incorporating as it did demands for workmen's compensation, old-age pensions, taxation of land values, 'popular' control over the drink trade and, of course, Irish Home Rule. Wheatley was certainly active in the campaign for Sullivan and was the leading speaker at an eve of poll meeting in Shettleston under the O'Connell branch's auspices. This endorsed in full the candidate's programme and called for the maximum of

Irish support for him.

Immediately before the dissolution of Parliament at the end of 1905, the League's London-based executive had issued a directive urging support for Labour candidates provided they held sound views on Irish Home Rule and were not standing against Liberals with well-established Home Rule credentials. Labour, however, won only two seats in Scotland: one the Glasgow Blackfriars seat with Irish support; and the other in Dundee, where the local UIL branches chose to back the Liberal candidate. This strategy received the eloquent blessing of John Ferguson, who had always made his political base the Glasgow Home Government branch of the old Parnellite National League and its successor the UIL, but was no sectarian in politics or religion. In 1883 the Glasgow Trades Council endorsed his campaign to secure election as a city councillor for the Calton ward, and he created a recognisable Labour council group which Wheatley was later to join.

The precise point at which Wheatley left the League has never been clear. R. K. Middlemas, in his book *The Clydesiders,* credited Wheatley with leaving the League and joining the ILP in 1907, but an obituary notice written in the very paper which he owned mentioned him joining the ILP in 1908. This was wrong, since Wheatley stood for the ILP in Shettleston as a Lanark County Council candidate in 1907 and appears to have been active in the local ILP branch before that, judging by the Shettleston ILP's minute books for the period. He was taking the chair at meetings at the start of 1907, and was elected branch chairman in March 1908. A minute for late April mentions another member taking the chair 'in the absence of Comrade Wheatley who was in Cambuslang spreading Socialism'.[4] The branch was an active one politically and socially, with its meetings well attended and good sales of Socialist literature organised by Wheatley's brother Patrick, and, by 1910, it had its own meeting hall in Shettleston which could also be let out to other organisations.

The first clear evidence of Wheatley proclaiming his social-ism occurred in the immediate aftermath of Labour's first breakthrough in the general election of 1906, in the form of a letter by him to the *Glasgow Observer* in February 1906, in reply to a lecture given at the Athenaeum Hall under the auspices of the Catholic Truth Society. The lecturer, one C. S. Devas, had elaborated the distinction that he believed to exist between the innocuous socialism of the new Labour MPs which posed no threat to faith, and the anti-Christian socialism exemplified by an agitator like Robert Blatchford and his paper the *Clarion*. Signing his letter 'Catholic Socialist', Wheatley made it clear that he did not see the lecture simply as a peace offering to the new Labour party and an assurance that Catholics might in conscience support it. He replied to Devas in a way that marked the onset of an extended attempt by him to prove the compatibility of his own increasingly militant socialism with a Catholic faith which he never doubted. Essentially, Wheatley argued that the whole ethos of Catholic Christianity was collec-tivist and concerned to root out inequality and social injustice: 'The Catholic church has always leaned more to socialism or collectivism and equality, than to individualism and inequality. It has always been the church of the poor and all the historical attacks on it have emanated from the rich. Its Divine Founder on every occasion condemned the accumulation of wealth.'[5] He quoted widely from Catholic writing to support his case and spoke of the Protestant reformation as a movement motivated by the gospel of acquisitive self-aggrandisement, helping to legitimise societies which destroyed faith by the very injustice and poverty that were part of them.

A socialism which eschewed the appearance or the reality of being anti-clerical and irreligious, like so many continental socialist parties, could work only to the long-term benefit of the church. Wheatley's own faith had survived the harsh poverty of his Baillieston childhood and the nightmare of the pits, but he made no assumptions about that of others. For him, true faith for the many could depend only on political action to raise them from a poverty often worse than that which he and his family had endured as first-generation immigrants. All this confirmed him in the support already taking shape in his own mind for the socialism of a political labour movement which, by 1908, had established both a secure relationship with the trade unions and a presence in Parliament.

One writer who certainly influenced that movement was Robert Blatchford, and Wheatley referred in 1906 to his *Britain for the British* as a major influence upon him. Blatchford was a prolific writer, whose work had a big sale, but his rejection of *laissez-faire* and Free Trade never took him much beyond an economic nationalism which many of Wheatley's socialist contemporaries found suspect. Wheatley's own critics were later to claim that there was more than a hint of this in his own analysis of the failures of the British economy after 1918.

He was certainly also impressed by the work of Francesco Nitti, an Italian political economist who, in 1891, had published a book on Catholic socialism. Four years later this was translated into English and represented a major synthesis of Catholic writing on the nature of poverty and class relationships. The burden of Nitti's argument was the tenuous moral basis for private property ownership, the need for Christians to hold goods in common, if need be through the moral agency of the collectivist state. Nitti's book, it has been argued, would not in its own right have converted Wheatley, but it seems to have reinforced decisively other influences which had reached him through his reading and, most vitally, to have wedded them to the faith passed on by his parents and Father Terken at St Bridget's. *Rerum Novarum*, the great social encyclical of Pope Leo XIII, had, in fact, rejected socialism as an answer to social problems, but it had analysed these problems at least from the standpoint of moral law and church teaching on matters like the living wage and working-class rights of association. In this sense, *Rerum Novarum* was vital in marking out areas of disagreement among Catholics like Wheatley and those clergy who sought to portray the socialism they espoused as a mortal danger to faith itself.

Wheatley was not in any sense a pioneer in the task of reconciling the gospel of radical social action with profound Christian convictions. The Labour movement in Britain would never have come into existence without the belief, particularly strong among Nonconformist Christians, that this could, and must, be done. His task was perhaps a harder one, coming as he did from a church with a tradition of formidable sanctions against intellectual dissent within its own ranks. The task consumed Wheatley's energies to the point where he was accused of giving Marxism less than its due as a significant intellectual tradition and a tool of analysis. This was later the view of Willie Gallacher, looking back on a period of close co-operation with Wheatley before his own decision to join the British Communist Party. He remembered Wheatley as an honest and worthy socialist blinkered, as he saw it, by his Catholicism from true ideological understanding, a recollection similar to that of another legendary Clydeside militant, Harry McShane. McShane, himself born a Catholic, admired Wheatley as a man of courage and conviction but, like Gallacher, felt that ultimately there was always a barrier between him and committed Marxists. This was why, in his reckoning, there was never any rapport between Wheatley and John MacLean. Indeed, McShane recalls a meeting at which Wheatley, from the chair, chose to interrupt an exposition of dialectical materialism by

MacLean to remind him that he was addressing a mainly Catholic audience. MacLean's reply was that his exposition would have been the same to a Protestant audience, but McShane saw the exchange as proof of a barrier between two gifted men.

What may well have sustained Wheatley in his first steps away from the politics of an essentially liberal Irish nationalism was the ambivalence of church pronouncements on socialism, often from Jesuit pulpits and platforms. These were frequently interspersed with apparent endorsement of the legitimate claims of a labour movement that was drawing an increasing part of its impetus from socialist doctrine. The predominantly working-class League of the Cross in Glasgow in September 1906 heard their Archbishop, Charles Maguire, welcoming the advent of the working class as a political force in its own right, while a notable Franciscan, Father David, felt able to tell a questioner at one of his lectures (who might well have been Wheatley) that since the church had not condemned the ILP, Catholics were free in conscience to join it.

It may have been shortly after this that Wheatley did indeed join the ILP, and, in doing so, he committed his political future to a body which, since its formation in 1893, had been a vigorous partner in the Labour coalition. Scottish socialists who had been involved in Keir Hardie's celebrated Mid-Lanark parliamentary contest of 1888 had willingly enough merged their separate Scottish Labour Party with the ILP in 1894 without trading off Scottish Home Rule as one of its central policies. When Wheatley joined in Shettleston, the ILP *was* Labour.

An equally important step, however, was his decision to found a Catholic Socialist Society (CSS) in Glasgow in November 1906. Some fifty members were enrolled at its first two meetings – actual membership, it appears, being confined to practising Catholics, though meetings normally held on Sunday afternoons in public halls or theatres, were open to all. The Society never had a large membership, perhaps a hundred or so at the most, but it maintained an active existence until after the First World War. Wheatley's press contacts secured it regular coverage in *Forward*, where a regular entry, 'Catholic Socialist Notes', often written by Wheatley himself, provided a good record of the Society's activities. These were not exclusively political, extending to dramatic readings and entertainments by pianists and singers, and, in the summer, to a good deal of outdoor activity. An athletics team, for example, took the field on the society's behalf at the Glasgow Socialist Sports of 1912 held, it should be noted, at Ibrox park. Rambles and picnics indeed superseded meetings in the summer months and their therapeutic importance for people whose working hours gave them very little time away from the city should not be underestimated. One report to *Forward* of a summer outing to Busby Reservoir near Glasgow concluded: 'The sun had long since dipped beneath the horizon before the itinerants turned their faces towards the grey city.'[6]

The society's first meeting was preceded by a letter from Wheatley published in the *Glasgow Observer*, inviting the attendance of all Catholics interested in socialism and, in the chair at the inaugural meeting, he laid much stress on the creation of a body in which 'they would have socialism preached in an atmosphere free from any irreligious taint'.[7] By the end of the month, after an initial series of meetings, Wheatley was able to write optimistically of the society's progress: 'Sunday after Sunday the attendance is good and the vigorous discussion that follows each lecture indicates a healthy spirit of inquiry among Glasgow Catholics. To those who still cherish the old belief that socialism and Catholicism are necessarily antagonistic, this growing success should be food for thought.'[8] The society's

stated aims were often reiterated and began to appear within
the various publications it published. The restriction of membership to Catholics was reaffirmed, and it was to them that
the socialist gospel must be taken, but it was to be the gospel
as taught by the ILP: 'Socialism is defined as the public ownership of land and capital. This does not mean the abolition of all
private property. The Society is in hearty agreement and co-
operates with the ILP.'[9] A wide range of speakers appeared
before the society's meetings. James Donaldson, a famous
activist among Baillieston miners, was one, and another trade
unionist to become vastly more famous was James Larkin, who,
in 1908, critically dissected nationalist and Sinn Fein approach-
es to the Irish Question. A speaker on women's rights who put
the case for state-nurseries seems to have had an apathetic
response from the audience, but interestingly, a week or two
later, a Mrs J. D. Pearce appeared to hold her audience on the
theme of 'Awakening Womanhood'.[10] Her plea was not simply
for the vote but for a society of true partnership between men
and women. *The Glasgow Observer* noted the presence of 'many
ladies in the audience on this occasion'.[11]

These first meetings of the society may have prompted
Wheatley's major collision of views with the clergy when a
Jesuit, Father Ashton, wrote to the *Observer* to censure
Catholics guilty of propagating the politics of class conflict.
Ashton's tone towards Wheatley himself was fairly complimen-
tary, knowing as he must have that his allegiance to the church
was not in doubt. Compliments were conspicuous by their
absence from the writings of another Jesuit soon to take issue
with Wheatley over the society's work and his involvement in
it. This was Leo Puissant, parish priest at St James's church,
Muirkirk, a Belgian from a family with a strong clerical tradition who had made a similar impact on his working-class
Scottish parish to that of Father Terken in Baillieston. Puissant

was a partisan of Christian social reform, applied under ultimate church control through lay Catholic parties, for which he saw scope both in his native country and in Britain. He castigated Wheatley for confusing good Catholics by urging their allegiance to a socialism of the working class which could well be contaminated by secularism and unbelief, paving the way to 'a world with human stud-farms and nursery-pens: a world of vice and filth, without religion and without grace'.[12] This line of attack, and the abrasive and admonitory language in which it was couched, forced Wheatley onto ground already occupied in earlier conflicts, especially in Irish nationalist history, over the political authority of the church. Emancipation for Irish Catholics must, in his view, lie with the working class as a whole, through its trade unions and political organisations, and Puissant's objections to this, based on selective quotation from *Rerum Novarum*, led Wheatley to call in question the claims of that encyclical to *ex-cathedra status*.

A measure of fame, or perhaps notoriety, was Wheatley's reward for his readiness to join public battle with a Jesuit about where Catholic political loyalties ought to lie. Other clergy weighed in with anathemas against the society and its work, and much local publicity was given to the fact that a similar body in Leeds had been suppressed at the order of the local diocese. The Archdiocese of Glasgow, despite the publicity for Wheatley's polemical exchanges with Father Puissant, was not tempted to follow the example of Leeds, and indeed Archbishop Maguire had more than once welcomed the emergence of an independent political movement of the working class as a necessary answer to brutal poverty and social injustice. This welcome, in fact, he had reiterated in stirring language to a huge audience at the 1908 Eucharistic Congress in London. But Wheatley's temerity in publicly criticising a priest, and a Jesuit into the bargain, forced the Archbishop's hand, and in November 1908 he convened a Diocesan Committee on socialism.

The report of this committee played down socialist influence as a threat to faith in the diocese, but it did single out Wheatley, unjustly categorising him as 'a malcontent Catholic' prepared to invite unbelievers and rationalists to speak to the society he had been instrumental in creating. In the words of one historian who analysed this episode, Wheatley, 'in a manner more easily felt than stated, was that most dangerous foe, a heretic, an enemy within the citadel of faith from which the Church defied the world'.[13] In fact it was felt imprudent to single out Wheatley for any specific retribution. The committee went no further than calling for further consideration to be given to the socialist danger and possibly for a Catholic Workers Association to be formed to protect the faithful from any contagion reaching them from the weekly meetings of the CSS. It also scented danger in the pamphlets beginning to come out under Wheatley's name.

The first of these, appropriately in view of his background, was *How the Miners are Robbed*. This was a savage polemic, uncompromising in its rejection from first principles of the political economy of a capitalism which could dominate and exploit whole communities in the manner of the Lanarkshire coal companies. It came out in 1907 and was followed in 1909 by *Mines, Miners and Misery*, a document much more personal in its evocation of the sights, smells and unceasing hazards that were the daily existence for the men Wheatley had left behind him, hacking out their share of the almost 300 million tons of coal which the British pits were producing annually in the period before 1914:

> If a man is killed suddenly, or gradually worn down by evil conditions, another is waiting to take his place and the profit making is not interrupted. Horses cost money and so must be cared for;

but things are so arranged that human beings may be had for nothing and retained for their keep. This is all they receive: sufficient to enable them to continue working, to enable them to bring up children to serve their masters when the children's fathers have been sent to the workhouse or the grave.[14]

One immediate result of his controversies with the clergy was for Wheatley to commit his ideas to print for the first time in a leaflet which came out under the Catholic Socialist Society's auspices. Conditions of membership and a restatement of the society's aims were included in the leaflet, which was entitled *The Catholic Working Man*. Essentially this was a defence of the position Wheatley had already held against his clerical opponents, but shrewdly reinforced with wide-ranging quotations from the church fathers, Cardinal Manning and, perhaps most effectively in its immediate local context, Archbishop Maguire himself:

> Our Socialism is not confiscation nor robbery nor the destruction of family life, nor anything like what you have heard our opponents describe it. It differs from the Socialism condemned by the Pope in that it retains the right to own private property. It is simply a scheme to abolish poverty.[15]

He analysed at some length, and with eloquence, Irish experience under British rule in the homeland and as an exiled labour force, concluding that this experience could only have the effect of converting them ultimately to socialism. 'Almost every Irishman who understands Socialism is a Socialist',[16] he declared optimistically, and went on to define the Irish Question primarily in terms of its relationship to the needs of British capitalism. This was an analysis that left little room for the psychology of domination or of how working-class Ulster Protestants would relate to any unified Irish state.

Its inspiration, Wheatley made it clear, was something which, for him, emanated 'from that spirit of brotherhood which is ever present in the hearts of man but which is often suppressed by the struggle for existence'.[17] It was a socialism illuminated by these insights into its relationship to church teaching and moral law that Wheatley successfully defended in a long-remembered debate with Hilaire Belloc in November 1909, which was held in the Pavilion Theatre in Renfield Street in central Glasgow in order to house the large paying audience the Catholic Socialist Society had anticipated would be present. Wheatley acquitted himself so well in his dissection of Belloc's attack on socialism as a threat to both faith and individual liberty, that he can safely be said to have arrived securely on the scene as an effective and eloquent protagonist of a non-Marxist socialism which Catholics could in good faith espouse. The reality of poverty, he told his audience on this occasion, 'was the hidden people of slums and poor houses, filthy in body, foul in speech and vile in spirit, but of our own manufacture, for every member of this class was once an innocent child'.[18]

Wheatley was, by this time, well known in the East End of Glasgow, and his house in Shettleston was a meeting place where socialists could gather and exchange ideas. His advice could be decisive in influencing younger people. Patrick Dollan recalled attending regular discussions at Wheatley's house and also the work of the Shettleston and Carntyne Dramatic Club which, with Wheatley's backing and financial assistance, staged plays with a political message. The club broke even financially as well, though assistance with props from Wheatley's old church of St Bridget helped. Towards the end of 1906 Wheatley was reported as announcing a forty-pound profit from the club's productions. This money was passed on to the church at Shettleston, which he was by then attending, in order to provide it with Stations of the Cross and a new statue of St Patrick.

Between 1906 and 1912, however, he became increasingly aware of, and angered by, the hostility shown towards himself and his activities by the priest of St Mark's Carntyne parish, within the bounds of which he and his family lived. The priest, a Father Robert Paterson, was, indeed, the object of a complaint on this account by Wheatley to Archbishop Maguire. The priest defended himself in a correspondence that has already been usefully quoted elsewhere. Paterson claimed in a letter to the Archdiocese that Wheatley had a dangerous influence on the young people of the parish, taking them to socialist meetings straight on from Sunday mass, and getting them to assist in the sale around the locality of *Forward*: 'the man has lost his faith, if he ever had any, and is now, by selling papers attacking the church, an enemy of the church.'[19]

All this was in 1911 and was a foretaste of what was to come in the following year. The Archdiocese itself had not given any formal backing to the campaign against Wheatley, but censure, even from within the parish, was not something to be dismissed. Someone else who learnt what it could mean was John McGovern, a former employee of Wheatley, who had become a regular attender at the Catholic Socialist Society's meetings. McGovern's parents were Catholics from County Cavan and his father worked nearby at Parkhead Forge. By 1911, McGovern was engaged to be married, only to find his local priest in Shettleston, Father Andrew O'Brien, making strong representations to his fiancée's father about the dangers of marriage to a confessed socialist who associated with Wheatley. McGovern's marriage went ahead despite clerical disapproval, but there was no respite for him from Father O'Brien's strictures. McGovern later recalled having to listen to the following words from this priest after he had been named during the sermon: 'I remember the time when his life would not have been worth twopence, but I urge you to do him no physical injury. It is hard, I know, for you to tolerate him in your midst, but I pray to God that you may restrain yourselves.'[20] This was close to incitement of the congregation against him, and McGovern, with his wife in some distress, left before the sermon finished and did not return to Father O'Brien's or any other church for several years.

The following year saw Wheatley himself placed under Father O'Brien's spiritual jurisdiction as a result of a diocesan reorganisation which united the adjacent Carntyne and Shettleston parishes. There is evidence that Father O'Brien's heavy-handed autocracy within his parish was less than welcome to the Archdiocese; indeed, it had led to trouble over other matters. Yet he was a priest of considerable presence and undoubted scholarship, also of personal wealth inherited from a pawnbroking business, something which soon became ammunition to be used against him in his clash with Wheatley. At a point when it was clear that there would be no backing from the Archdiocese for an offensive against socialism in its East End parishes, O'Brien chose, in the early summer of 1912, to denounce both socialism and Wheatley himself in the most uncompromising language from his pulpit in St Paul's, Shettleston. Wheatley, who had attended mass with his wife, sat apparently unmoved through this diatribe, but later turned to the columns of *Forward* to defend himself. He pulled no punches in doing so, saying of Father O'Brien: 'One of his favourite poses is as the friend of God's poor. While God's poor are prepared to act like slaves and sycophants they are flattered, but independence is treated as a deadly sin.'[21] Wheatley arranged for extra copies of this issue of *Forward* to be distributed in the locality, while the local ILP branch arranged an open-air meeting in his support for Monday 1 July, near the town cross in Shettleston main street. Meanwhile, girls from the parish tore down *Forward* posters, and on

the Sunday it became clear that a vocal majority of the parishioners would support their priest. Only a few ILP members
turned up for the meeting at the cross, and were attacked by
an angry crowd. One member, Andrew Fleming, who sat on
the local school board, emerged from this fracas with a broken
nose. A crowd, by then numbering several hundred, moved on
down the street to Wheatley's house, where his two children
were at home with a friend, Daniel McAleer, and his wife.
McAleer was a local man who had made a similar transition to
Wheatley from Irish nationalist politics into the ILP and had
himself clashed with Father O'Brien. Wheatley had gone out
for an evening stroll with his wife, returning with her when
word reached him of the crowd who appeared to be threaten-
ing his home.

What happened subsequently has been described in various
accounts,[22] but the most determined section of the crowd had
an effigy of Wheatley which they burned outside his house to
the strains of the venerable Catholic hymn 'Faith of Our
Fathers'. This occupied an hour or so, and the cool courage
with which Wheatley, pipe in hand, confronted the crowd and
then walked through them unmolested was remembered long
afterwards. Whether there was a serious intention on the part
of Wheatley's fellow parishioners to ransack his house may be
doubted. A witness of the event, who later became for a time
Wheatley's secretary, thought not:

> To attack and wreck the home of a heretic living in a slum would
> have been child's play. To attack the house of a prominent citizen
> was another matter. All their inherent veneration and fear of the
> man of property came to the top. They knew by the accumulated
> experiences of generations of slave minds that the law protected
> property and men of property. They hesitated, wavering and
> undecided.[23]

Although no harm came from this episode and indeed his

own bearing in the face of possible real danger enhanced his reputation, it troubled Wheatley none the less that his political beliefs could have been used against him in such a way. The following Saturday his reactions appeared in *Forward* in the form of some questions put directly to the crowd who had threatened his home only four days previously:

> On Monday night you gathered in your hundreds or thousands to demonstrate that you hated me. If I am an enemy, am I your only enemy? Don't you know that God who gave you life has created for you green fields and sunny skies, that he has given you the material and the power to have in abundance beautiful homes, healthy food, education, leisure, travel and all that aids in the development of cultured men and women. These gifts of God have been stolen from you.[24]

How many of the effigy-burners were regular *Forward* readers is a matter for conjecture, but reaffirmation of his belief in human brotherhood and the fair sharing of God's bounty to the world shone through the way Wheatley reacted to an event which he might easily have exploited to win for himself an aura of cheap martyrdom.

The episode, though upsetting while it lasted, had few permanent effects. Wheatley and his wife were back at mass the following Sunday without incident, and Father O'Brien kept the charge until 1922, earning much goodwill for himself for his pastoral care for, and generosity to, the parish, notably to the many unemployed, not all of them Catholics, after the First World War. Later in 1912 Wheatley was elected by Shettleston to represent it as a councillor on the Glasgow Corporation, and three years later was a popular hero for his agitation on behalf of the evicted wives of soldiers from the area serving on the Western Front. On the latter occasion he was not averse to reminding a cheering crowd of the happenings in the street outside his home on 1 July 1912.

3 Local politics

Wheatley made his first bid for local office under ILP auspices when he stood, in 1907, for a vacant place on Lanarkshire County Council, but was heavily defeated by a local businessman who was also a Catholic. In 1910 Wheatley won the seat by just four votes in a bruising contest which centred upon dubious practices by the sitting councillor, who had secured tenders for a local hospital project for former employees of his building business who bought most of their materials from him. Some local priests were angered by Wheatley's intervention against a fellow Catholic and made their anger clear during the election campaign.

From the moment of his election Wheatley quickly earned a reputation as an active local councillor. There were few matters under the County Council's jurisdiction with which he did not concern himself, from drainage to local employees' wages. On domestic water supply, he won a substantial victory in council, forcing the Public Health Committee to agree to an annual inspection of the water storage tanks which it maintained to supply water to many of the houses in the ward. Such an inspection had not been carried out before and revealed appalling evidence of contamination, sometimes in the form of dead and decomposing rats in the tanks. The outcry which resulted from the publicity given by Wheatley to these revelations secured a commitment by the council to annual inspection, and he was able to use the whole episode in his campaign to have the incidence of consumption (tuberculosis) in the area properly documented. In fact, on the council's behalf, he attended major medical conferences on consumption and brought back to his colleagues lucid reports of what he had learnt. He saw, too, the inescapable connection between the disease's toll and standards of accommodation in the Lanarkshire coalfield, and he pressed for a Public Health Committee report on the type and size of house occupied by all registered victims in the area within the County Council's jurisdiction.

County Councils by this time were significant employers of labour, most of it unskilled, and Wheatley worked hard for the protection of workers doing heavy and dirty work such as refuse disposal. He secured a fair wage clause in their contract of employment as well as adequate washing facilities for them at the cleansing and disposal plants where much of their work was done. Street-sweepers and lamp-lighters (the latter celebrated in some children's verse by R. L. Stevenson, but no less vulnerable to exploitation because of it) also found Wheatley ready to take up their cause where working conditions and a living wage were concerned. The enactment of private legislation by Glasgow Corporation in 1912 cut short Wheatley's term as a County Councillor, but at the same time presented him with the much more challenging arena of Glasgow itself, for Shettleston and other outlying areas, including the burghs of Govan, Partick and Pollokshaws, were incorporated within the city's jurisdiction.

Shettleston's annexation by Glasgow was at first resisted locally, as such annexations had often been by peripheral localities during the period of Glasgow's municipal expansion, and a committee was formed to mobilise opposition and to put the local view to Glasgow Corporation (as the sponsor of the required private bill) and to Parliament. Ironically, perhaps, in view of the way Shettleston was to become his own political base within an enlarged municipality of Glasgow, Wheatley in fact gave some support to this agitation, though seemingly not really believing that Glasgow's wishes could be thwarted. Ultimately he retreated to the view that if annexation must go ahead, then Shettleston and adjacent Tollcross should be transferred as a single Ward.

After his work on the County Council and for the Catholic Socialist Society, Wheatley's adoption by the Shettleston ILP as their candidate was a formality, but the contest itself was one in which, his own Irishness and Catholicism notwithstanding, Wheatley had to face the censure of the *Glasgow Observer*. The paper was fundamentally well-disposed to Labour, and later went wholeheartedly over to it, but it was still preoccupied with what it viewed as Labour's reluctance to adopt Irish and Catholic candidates for local election to an extent that reflected the Catholic community's political importance. The Irish vote, the *Observer* claimed, held the balance in a dozen of the city's local wards, all the better reason for Labour responding in its actual nomination of candidates. Except for three Labour councillors seeking re-election, the paper's editorials urged readers to vote against Labour candidates, a 'deplorable necessity to show Labour it cannot disregard the Irish vote in the city; we are willing to be allies, we decline to be slaves.'[1] Labour's position was the simple one that Irish candidates could be supported only if they belonged to affiliated organisations. This the UIL was not; for, sympathetic to Labour as many of its branches clearly were, its prime commitment remained to the Liberal alliance in order to secure a Dublin Parliament.

Wheatley's firm base in Shettleston proved to be more important than any attempts from the *Glasgow Observer* or elsewhere to represent him as some kind of traitor to the Irish in Glasgow, and in the contest to fill the Shettleston and Tollcross ward's three seats, he came out top of the poll with 2,129 – a decisive victory, almost 55 per cent of the local electorate having voted. The City Chambers in which he took his seat was, and still is, a sumptuous structure, raised in the 1880s with vast expenditure on marble and mosaic and in imitation of what seems like half-a-dozen styles. Flight upon flight of balustraded stairs lead the way to spacious committee rooms, a banquet hall and the imposing Council Chamber itself – the whole a visible monument to the dynamic mercantile capital-ism which made Glasgow the second city of the British Empire, but at the price of immeasurable and avoidable human misery. It was, in many ways, a cosmopolitan city which could boast artists and designers of avant-garde taste and could play host to the world at lavish exhibitions in 1888, 1901 and 1911, housed on huge sites and attracting millions of visitors. By the time of this third exhibition, Glasgow's prosperity was existing on borrowed time, but, for the minority of the popu-lation (perhaps 25 per cent) who were middle class, the city's West End and its southern suburbs afforded a life-style of enormous affluence.

It was a much-governed city, too, and by any contemporary standards a well-governed one, which had built up a wide range of municipal services. By 1912 these covered water, gas, electricity, a tramway system and a telephone service, and an Improvement Trust had existed since 1866 with comprehensive slum clearance (but not house-building) powers. There was also an energetic Public Health Department, and a Police Department, whose powers extended to the designation of, or 'ticketing' and clearing of overcrowded houses. All this put the Liberal business men and lawyers who ran Glasgow into a position of some embarrassment when commentators abroad described the city as a laboratory of municipal enterprise, even of local authority socialism. Commentators on city government and politics, when writing on Glasgow, often raised the ques-tion of precisely how much political or ideological content there was in the city's municipal collectivism, and argued that successive councils and administrators had simply made a pragmatic response to pressing visible problems created by rapid urban growth. *The Times*, in October 1902, included Glasgow in a series of lengthy articles on municipal socialism in British cities, and the then Lord Provost felt obliged to clear the city's name from association with the title of the series. He was at particular pains to deny that the council was moving towards municipal housing or that the Improvement Trust had ever been conceived of as a step towards municipal house-building for the working class: 'The idea of the corporation undertaking a scheme for the direct purpose of accommodating the poor had not dawned upon the municipality nor on the public,'[2] he insisted.

Skilled workers in more secure employment, from whose ranks were to come many of the militants who created the legend of the 'Red Clyde', tended to get longer leases, sometimes a full year, on the better tenement properties; for the rest, incomers in insecure or casual work, the low-paid and the unemployed, Scots law on house tenancy and rent arrears made life a constant struggle for survival against property owners and house factors. 'The silent struggle between landlord and tenant was fought with a peculiar savagery in Glasgow,'[3] it has been said, and evictions for arrears or non-payment continued until 1914 at a level far above that of other cities of comparable size.

Glasgow was equipped with a formidable range of statutory powers to deal with insanitary and overcrowded housing, but none of these powers was used to the full, and certainly not if doing so meant the eviction of families without the guarantee of alternative accommodation. This, indeed, was the brutal paradox of Victorian Glasgow's housing legacy: the very rate at which the problem grew created humanitarian aversion to a full use of the powers belonging to the municipality. The vicious circle was thus completed and could be broken only when commercial and ideological resistance to large-scale construction by the corporation was overcome.

Once elected, Wheatley could give more time to council work than many of his Labour colleagues, and accepted nomination to a total of eight committees, including those concerned with Health, Tramways and the City Improvement Trust. His first formal motion was to challenge a minute concerning salary increases for two civic officials, and his speech on this occasion earned him early, if less than ecstatic, notice from the press. 'Among our new members who threaten to take up a good deal of our time, Mr Wheatley has made his start.'[4] The most important debate in Wheatley's first year as a councillor was undoubtedly that prompted by Lord Provost Stevenson in April 1913. Stevenson's motion was for an executive committee on housing to be formed by the council to carry out all the powers the corporation had under existing housing legislation and to close and demolish all houses that were a hazard either to safety or to health. Wheatley sought to press an amendment that the committee, if set up, must have the authority to rehouse people displaced by its demolition work and to subsidise rents for the poorest of the city's families. The debate was a wide-ranging one, though in the end Wheatley agreed to withdraw his own amendments to assist the carrying of the Lord Provost's motion.

Although he was active over a wide range of issues that came before the council, it was on housing that he made his mark. Labour pressure before the 1912 elections had succeeded in securing a special committee to consider the use of corporation ground to build rented cottages for the working class, and in April 1913 this committee produced a report costing an experimental scheme in one area, Riddrie. Its recommendations were rejected by the council by a large majority, with

Wheatley and the Labour councillors being among the twenty-seven who voted in favour. The exact powers and functions of the new executive committee on housing were a matter of some dispute and, indeed, divided the council so evenly as to require the Lord Provost to use a casting vote. This arose from a minute by the committee seeking powers to purchase, in its own right, slum property in designated 'congested areas'. The legality of such spending powers in a committee's hands was called in question by the Town Clerk, whose doubts were strongly backed by Wheatley. Accusations soon followed that the minute was merely giving the city's slum landlords a respectable façade for doing business with the municipality without the full council being consulted. Feeling ran so high that two Labour councillors were suspended by the Lord Provost and police were called in when they refused to leave the chamber.

Wheatley had been an active participant in this controversy, which had certainly been used by the Labour group to make its presence felt in the Council Chamber, and a few months later he attracted much more attention by leading a Labour onslaught on the role of the city's Victorian Improvement Trust. He characterised the trust as a parasitic body which had spent heavily on clearing designated areas, but with minimal results in terms of any additions to the city's housing stock. His concern with housing stemmed directly from his own experience of what gross overcrowding and defective sanitation had meant in Lanarkshire pit villages like Baillieston. He now lived in rented ground-floor accommodation just off Shettleston High Street and was later to become a house owner, but housing never ceased to preoccupy him as a matter deserving to be highest in Labour's priorities. He was not satisfied either with merely attacking the complacency of the council, for he worked hard on a scheme of his own to provide rented hous-

ing which working- class tenants could afford and which would
be financed from the large surplus earned by the Tramway
Department. This rested on the view that where social need
was concerned, local revenues were indivisible and that workers' cottages could be built with a non-interest-bearing loan
from the Tramway Department.

Later in 1913, Wheatley found a more important forum for
his housing views in the Royal Commission on the Housing of
the Industrial Population of Scotland. He used the questions
put to him as a witness in order to restate the Glasgow Labour
group's policy, above all the crying need for local authority
intervention to provide the bulk of working-class housing. He
also restated his scheme for funding cheap cottages from the
Tramway surplus, and pressed the case for local councils,
Glasgow's in particular, to buy up new land for houses on the
city boundaries. This policy, when implemented, would lead in
the longer term to some planning disasters beyond Wheatley's
imagination. His concern was, and remained, with housing on
a human scale which would preserve what was best in working-class community living.

Challenged by some of the commissioners, Wheatley denied
that working-class housing at reduced costs to tenants would
tempt employers to cut wages, and argued the municipal
socialist case for large local authorities to compete with private
enterprise. When this happened, he maintained, wages would
cease to be determined by mere subsistence.[5] Taken overall,
his performance before the commission was agreed to have
been a competent one, though where he faltered was on the
question of how tenants would be selected. His questioner put
to him the problem of the brutalising effects of poverty on
some of the casually employed and very poor, and whether
they would qualify for leases of council-built homes. Wheatley
let his Labour council colleague, James Stewart, answer the

question, which he did essentially in terms of the need to discipline such tenants by appropriate sanctions. The suggestion that Wheatley's concern with housing was to protect the respectability of skilled workers in regular employment rather than to meet the needs of the very poorest would be heard again when he became Minister of Health and Housing in 1924.

He had already argued the case for his scheme at a series of public meetings, the City Labour Party adopted it, and volunteer speakers were appealed for to explain it to all Labour, ILP, Co-Operative and trade union branches throughout the city. His 1913 pamphlet, *Eight-Pound Cottages for Glasgow Citizens*, was therefore an important weapon in a campaign for a radical change in the city's housing policy, and it reveals, too, the careful way in which Wheatley prepared any case. The damning evidence of strikingly different death rates and consumption levels between working-class and residential areas was vividly documented. In some areas, he declared, tenement slums were the slaughter houses of the poor, who died at a rate per 1,000 of three, four and sometimes five times the frequency of those in the West End or the newer residential suburbs. Yet out of this inequality and multiple deprivation he believed a 'greater and grander' Glasgow could arise: 'By sustained united effort the democracy could raise a city which would be a worthy monument to the capture of civic power by the common people.'[6]

Wheatley came to personify for many people the Glasgow labour movement's concern with housing, but that concern, of course, had been central to Labour and especially to ILP thinking while Wheatley's first allegiance was still to the United Irish League. As far back as its 1902 Liverpool Conference the ILP had debated the financing of local authority house-building, which was an integral element of party policy well before Wheatley achieved any prominence in Glasgow. His contribution was not, therefore, in forcing housing to the top of the ILP's agenda, but in focusing attention on the experience of housing policy in some continental cities and in arguing in his pamphlets and speeches for an original approach to the funding of new housing.

Recent extensions of the city's municipal boundaries had, in some ways, worsened the problems of high population density and overcrowding. He cited city councils abroad, notably in Germany, as proof of the benefits accruing to the community when local government was persuaded to buy up building land and to apply tight 'zoning' policies and control over building developments. In Glasgow's case, using the Tramway Department's surplus to fund a real attack on the housing problem was something Wheatley felt he could justify as a simple capital transfer exercise, the capital in question being an asset belonging to the people of Glasgow. From there he went on to a detailed costing of an exercise which could, he argued, provide houses and cottages at annual rents below the average being paid presently by the city tenant to private owners. The whole campaign and the pamphlet to publicise it linked Wheatley's name permanently with the advocacy of challenging alternatives to housing policies which, in Glasgow and elsewhere, were a literal death sentence on the many poor.

Wheatley's period as a councillor was an important political staging point for him, for it marks decisively his move away from the politics of Irish nationalism, but he was not in 1914 a convert to any centralist belief in the British state as an instrument of socialist advance. Indeed, his council work drew him to the belief that energetic municipal action by socialists could, if widely enough diffused, make the role of the state redundant. He could write with eloquence of a civic, decentralised socialist future, in the attainment of which Glasgow could lead the way. This phase in his thinking was cut short by the brutal imperatives of a war which added vastly to an apparatus of state power which he quickly decided socialists would have to come to terms with. By 1914, Wheatley had become a figure to reckon with in the Labour movement in Glasgow, and his management of a successful and expanding business gave him an important measure of control over his time, no small consideration when other Labour councillors could claim no entitlement to be absent from their employment on municipal business. His regular contributions to *Forward* enhanced the reputation he earned in the Council Chamber, and he continued to find time for more general statements of political belief, like his 1912 pamphlet, *A Christian in Difficulties*.

In some ways this was a development of the credo he had set out in his 1909 pamphlet, *The Catholic Working Man*, but he presented it as the odyssey through a world corrupted by greed of an apocryphal 'Martin Maynes', a committed Christian who seeks to maintain his own standards in a world where, in practice, they are held in low regard. 'Maynes' begins as owner of a business in which he seeks to pay a living wage to his employees, only to be undercut by 'sweaters' who mock his scruples. Other ventures bring him up against dishonest trading, adulterated food, stolen and shoddy goods knowingly marketed, and a pool of surplus labour wantonly and relentlessly exploited in the interest of wider profit margins. Wheatley wrote, of course, as an entrepreneur whose own business methods had certainly been robust, on his own admission, but he could still react fiercely against 'an order of things in which moral and material waste is profitable and virtue severely taxed'.[7] Such a system, he wrote, 'is damned and should be destroyed. . . He alone is practical who strives for a state of society in which all will gain by the virtue of each.'[8]

His increasing commitment to local council work did not dilute in Wheatley's mind the great importance of the link he represented between the Catholic community and a political labour movement increasingly socialist in its objectives. He continued to attend the Catholic Socialist Society's regular Sunday meetings as often as he could, sometimes to lecture or to take the chair, and he was willing to take the society's case to ordinary branch meetings of the United Irish League with which he retained many contacts.

The Wheatley home in Shettleston had a political atmosphere, and his son later recalled the constant traffic of visitors brought there by his father's reputation. One frequent caller was Tom Bell, a young syndicalist iron-moulder active in the small Socialist Labour Party and later a founder of the British Communist Party. Although he enjoyed debates at the Wheatley home, he came to fear his host's ability to win over to the ILP waverers from the other socialist groups. Another visitor was James Connolly, for whom, after his return to Scotland in 1910 from a period in the USA, Wheatley arranged a series of meetings under the auspices of both the Glasgow Clarion Scouts (a group organised around the socialist paper of the same name) and the Catholic Socialist Society.

The arrival of Connolly in Glasgow, and the formation of Sinn Fein branches in the city as a militant alternative to the constitutional Home Rule politics of the UIL, were a reminder to Wheatley of the Irish allegiance which first took him into politics. His move into activism within the labour movement was a shift in his priorities as an Irishman in Scotland, and arose partly, too, from unease at the continuing closeness of the Irish Nationalist Party's alliance with the Liberals, but he had not abandoned his Irish identity. The CSS frequently discussed Ireland, and the 1910 general election and the passage of the Parliament Act, knocking away as it did the last constitutional obstacle to Home Rule, gave added urgency to the formulation of an Irish policy within the society, in *Forward*, and in the labour movement as a whole.

Wheatley's own view did not diverge from that of the labour movement, namely to give all necessary support to the Liberal government's resurrected Home Rule legislation. Through the mounting crisis of Conservative and Ulster Loyalist resistance to this legislation, his view remained consistent. He was bitterly opposed to even temporary partition to meet the Loyalists' demands, since this 'would divide the democracy of Ireland into two hostile camps',[9] a view he maintained after partition had become a reality.

As already stressed, Wheatley's clashes with individual clergy over his socialism in no way affected his own faith, except perhaps to strengthen it. He continued to attend mass in the same church where he had been denounced from the pulpit, and a lingering whispering campaign against him appeared to have as little effect as the effigy-burning crowd which had briefly threatened his home. The education of his own children may be cited here, since he and his wife could have enrolled their son John and their daughter Elizabeth at the local Board school. The Catholic church, however, had taken care to keep its own, mostly elementary, schools outwith the jurisdiction and also the funding of the school Boards, and it was to the local Catholic elementary school in Shettleston that both children went. Depending as they did on voluntary support along with what central government was prepared to make over in an annual grant, such schools often had a struggle, intensified by the often dire poverty of many of the families whose children they sought to educate. It was this as much as anything that militated against the Catholic system's ability to develop much beyond the elementary level and created a dilemma for Wheatley. The Board system certainly offered a wider choice of school at secondary level, though for many Catholics what it seemed to offer, or indeed to threaten, was either secularism or thinly veiled denominationalism in the form of religious knowledge classes and worship conducted by Church of Scotland members.

Wheatley and his wife appear to have had few doubts, therefore, about enrolling their daughter at the private Notre Dame Girls' High School, and their son at St Aloysius. The latter, founded by Jesuits in 1859 as a fee-paying boys' day school, took pupils right through from elementary instruction to secondary, and in time acquired a considerable reputation and began to appeal to all Catholic parents who had the financial means to take up places for their sons. St Aloysius, indeed, contributed to the social mobility of the Irish community in Scotland in this century, for its fees were not prohibitive to those successful in business, like Wheatley, or profitably self-employed in the professions which second- and third-generation Irish began to penetrate. The longer term and larger issue of segregating Catholic children within their own school system does not appear to have exercised Wheatley, concerned though he was at a practical political level to oppose religious sectarianism and make the labour movement's socialism a common cause for Catholic and non-Catholic. It must be said, too, that he was not the last socialist to invest in a private education for his own family, though his choice might have been different had he been required to make it after the legislation of 1918 which brought the Catholic schools (but not St Aloysius and a few others) into the existing state system.

Wheatley's son, who went on to university and then entered the family business, looking back across the years to his childhood in Shettleston, remembered a great deal of personal happiness amidst the constant bustle of political activity centering on, and emanating from, the family home. Inevitably the affairs of Hoxton and Walsh, council business and the unceasing demands of meetings and lectures kept Wheatley away a good deal, but never to the point where he ceased to be a father to his son and daughter, and a loving one too. His wife, Mary, hardly seems to emerge from a position overshadowed by her husband's increasing political stature; whether she even wished to, we cannot know. Her son remembers her for her warmth and kindness. Self-effacing she may have been, with few aspirations independent of her husband, but she was a source of support and comfort which may have given her more influence than she knew.

John Wheatley had acquired the political leverage that he had in Glasgow and in the labour movement of 1914 without the personal magnetism sometimes imagined to be a requirement of those who build and lead socialist movements. John MacLean may ultimately have been a failure, but a charismatic failure whose words and presence held people and haunted them long afterwards. Maxton, incorruptible and courageous like MacLean, had a presence made dramatic by his cadaverous looks and famously long hair. ('What about the unemployed barbers, Jimmy?', good-humoured hecklers used to call out at his meetings.) Wheatley, twenty years older, was in a real sense Maxton's mentor, as indeed he may have been of others, but their recollections of him before 1914 all confirm the absence of qualities that create legends. They recall a fastidious dresser, tending to corpulence, the epitome, John Paton thought, of the successful business man whose career would have commended itself to Samuel Smiles. His voice was not a compelling one, if anything high-pitched for the purposes of the strenuous outdoor propaganda which he and Patrick Dollan had undertaken years before in and around Baillieston among robustly critical audiences. Perseverance reaped its own reward and, coupled with a sharp and receptive mind, made him not perhaps a great orator but a debater never to be underestimated. 'He wore thick glasses which added to his mild and benevolent appearance', Willie Gallacher recalled, 'but behind the glasses was a pair of keen, watchful eyes that spoke of a brain ever active and subtle.'[10] The debating style which remained his own and stood him in good stead in Labour conferences and in Parliament was the one he shaped in this period and has been described in some vivid detail:

> He still emphasizes his argument by a characteristic striking of the open palm of the left hand with two fingers of the right. As the argument develops the hand moves proportionately quicker, until reaching its climax. The last movement is the most interesting of all. He seems to feel that his opponents are in the hollow of that left hand, and when the last argument is shattered the two fingers are swished along the open palm with a movement which gives the impression that both opponents and arguments are being swept to the floor and finally disposed of.[11]

People listened to Wheatley and learned from him at a time of intense political activity among skilled workers in Glasgow. They were avid for the stimulus of new ideas and challenges to preconceptions relayed to them, whether by churches, employers or press lords. One young Glaswegian worker, eager for self-education and beginning to doubt his inherited Catholicism, was Harry McShane. He used to await avidly Wheatley's contributions to *Forward* and the *Glasgow Observer*, attended many of his meetings and admired his work as a Labour councillor: 'He never claimed to be a Marxist but I sometimes felt he was more of a Marxist than some who claimed to be.'[12] McShane's perception here may have been less than accurate, though intended as a compliment for all that. He recognised in John Wheatley a man of courage, who wanted to use his talents and the modest wealth they had won for him to destroy the poverty from which he had escaped: and to change society in the image of God rather than of Marx.

4 War and the Red Clyde

The world of active socialists in Glasgow before 1914 was a small one but charged with a real sense of cultural aspiration and attainable change, even though the city was still a strongly Liberal one both in its local and parliamentary politics. The city's labour force was, moreover, divided between skilled and unskilled workers, while in some localities and industries, like the shipyards, a tenacious subculture of Orange Toryism mocked the crusading efforts of socialists. Yet there was also, in 1914, a new generation of skilled workers ready to hold their ground against increasingly autocratic company managements committed to using technological change and fluctuating demand as weapons to break such strength as organised labour had achieved.

War altered radically the contours of this local battleground, yet its advent was conceived of by most socialists as something unthinkable and irrational, the product of great power jealousies and capitalist intrigues which workers acting together across frontiers could expose for what they were. Whether workers in Glasgow had the will or the political resources to do this was put to the test from 4 August 1914 onwards.

In Glasgow, as in many other places, the working class supported the war with an initial enthusiasm which subsided into a dour belief, hardened by its own sacrifices, that the struggle must be seen through to some sort of ultimate victory over Germany and its allies. The initial enthusiasm should not be doubted, however. The Highland Light Infantry alone,

Glasgow's own regiment, raised twenty-six battalions from the city; one of them recruited the volunteers it needed from the Tramway Department's employees in just sixteen hours.

Labour had nineteen councillors in the City Chambers in 1914, but only two of these opposed the declaration of war by Britain. They were John Wheatley and John S. Taylor, and not until conscription came did the Labour group as a whole adopt a position of support for a negotiated peace with the Central Powers. Wheatley's initial minority position was almost a replica of the situation in the Parliamentary Labour Party which, of course, was why Ramsay MacDonald resigned from its chairmanship after the outbreak of the war.

Wheatley and Taylor acted in conformity with the anti-war stance of the ILP, whose National Administrative Council, comprising MacDonald, Keir Hardie, Snowden and others, condemned the war in memorable and uncompromising language:

> Out of the darkness and the depth we hail our working class comrades of every land. Across the roar of the guns, we send sympathy and greetings to the German Socialists. They have laboured unceasingly to promote good relations with Britain, as we with Germany. They are no enemies of ours, but faithful friends.[1]

Forward, though its later attitude to war resistance was accused by some of being equivocal, portrayed the outbreak of war as darkness descending on civilisation. Sir Edward Grey was denounced for subservience to the interests of the Tsarist tyranny in Russia, and its front page ran a cartoon of a bloated top-hatted speculator squatting on a pile of hoarded food alongside a gruesome Boer War photograph of a trench on Spion Kop choked with British corpses.

Wheatley shared this view and was among the speakers on 9 August at an ILP rally on Glasgow Green to which the city's

Trades Council gave its backing, though only by a narrow majority of forty-six to thirty-five. His speech to an audience of some 5,000 people, interrupted at times by a Territorial Army band billeted at the People's Palace nearby, was much taken up with the field-day war would provide for profiteers and price manipulators unless prompt action was taken to secure social control of the distribution of food and other essentials, and the meeting carried a resolution to that effect. A strength of the anti-war campaign in Glasgow was indeed that it never lost touch with the need to focus the war's effects on local problems, while the Union of Democratic Control, with its programme confined to a negotiated peace without annexations and open diplomacy, never made a large impact in Glasgow. Wheatley, however, did attend the opening of its Glasgow branch, when MacDonald spoke with power and eloquence.

David Kirkwood, who was also present, wrote later: 'That night John Wheatley and I became Ramsay MacDonald's men.'[2] MacDonald's principled call for a negotiated end to the war, and the savage attacks it drew upon him, certainly won him the admiration of many anti-war socialists in Glasgow and there is no reason to doubt that Wheatley was one of them. Yet working-class patriotism was never something Wheatley mocked. Indeed, he was realist enough to see it as more than merely an aberrant and inconvenient phenomenon which social-ists could simply hustle off the political stage. What he resent-ed, however, was the way he saw a genuine emotion being exploited with no guarantees for the protection of working-class families from the real hardship of losing wage-earners on war service. As early as August 1914 he sought, amidst angry interruptions in the council, to block a scheme for raising local civic battalions unless adequate provision from local funds was assured for the families of those who joined up under the scheme.

He turned his fire as well on attempts by the authorities to convert voluntary recruitment into a veiled form of compulsion. By the autumn of 1915 the Coalition government was under fierce pressure to abandon voluntaryism and Lord Derby, himself a conscriptionist, was commissioned with the task of organising a scheme by which men of military age would 'attest' their willingness to serve when called upon. It was an alternative to immediate call-up for those who had not yet answered Lord Kitchener's accusing posters, though pressure to attest could be strong:

> Squire nagged and bullied, I went
> to fight, under Lord Derby's scheme

were words Siegfried Sassoon later gave to a soldier in one of his war poems. In Glasgow, the council endorsed the Derby scheme, and agreed to special allowances for city employees who attested. A special committee on recruitment agreed that these allowances be paid only to men who had actually attested by 30 November 1916. This was carried in the face of Wheatley's opposition to what he described as a crude method of pressurising those who had not yet joined up with the loss of a civic allowance to their families: it was part and parcel of a policy prevalent all over the country of trying to have conscription under the façade of voluntaryism.

Opposition to the Derby scheme was only the start of the fight against conscription. Wheatley supported this campaign, and used the council as a forum for pressing the case, clashing angrily with the majority and the Lord Provost over the anti-conscriptionists' right to use municipal premises for their meetings. This issue, in fact, led to Wheatley and ten other Labour councillors being suspended from the Chamber, but the campaign went on, strengthened in January 1918 by a ninety to three vote in the Trades Council against the Military Service Bill.

Wheatley's anti-war stance was a principled one which he showed himself ready to justify against the Labour leadership, the noisy patriots who controlled industry and local government, and against his own church, for Archbishop Charles Maguire used his pulpit in Glasgow's Catholic cathedral not merely to urge his congregation to enlist but also to call upon priests of military age to do the same. As 'Catholic Socialist Notes' put it in *Forward*: 'We are assured that if Christ lived today he would don the patriotic khaki and place his services unreservedly at the disposal of Kitchener.'[3] For Wheatley this was a bitter moment, since the Archbishop's views on many social questions were ones with which he could identify, but he did not let it influence his own attitude to the continuation of the war.

Whether objective conditions existed for a campaign to defeat conscription by making it unworkable on Clydeside may be doubted. The supposition that they did, and that the need was simply for more agitators of the calibre of John MacLean to exploit them, is a necessary part of the 'Red Clyde' legend. More immediate prospects of a tangible working-class victory materialised over an issue on which Wheatley as pamphleteer and councillor had already secured his credentials as an expert: housing and rents.

Rising interest rates, along with added pressure on housing from war workers pouring into Clydeside, tempted many of the city's property owners to seek general rent increases and to enforce them with their traditional weapon of eviction. Within barely a week of the outbreak of war, Wheatley sought to alert the council to the danger of the housing shortage being exploited in this way. Agreement was reached on the council to make representations to the city's Property Owners and House Factors Association, but events soon showed what little effect these representations actually had.

The City Labour Party and its councillors were well placed

to lead any impending struggle over rents, having already, partly under Wheatley's influence, developed radical housing policies to be funded initially from the profits of successful city enterprises like the tramways. Labour continued its propaganda for these schemes, though in the knowledge that the council was unlikely to adopt them from simple gratitude for the patriotic response to the war of the city's working class. In fact, in early 1915 the permanent property owners' majority on the council had their position secured by the Town Clerk's ruling that it would be illegal to use funds from one local department to finance the expenditure of another.

Predictable rejection by the council did not affect Labour's commitment to local authority housing as the central element in its policy. Indeed, when the wartime rent increases first began to bite in early 1915, identification over several years with this commitment gave both Labour and the Glasgow Women's Housing Association, formed in late 1914, an all-important credibility among tenants in the areas worst affected by the increases. Recent accounts of the 1915 rent campaign make clear the extent to which it was a Labour Party campaign rather than one controlled by the Clyde Workers Committee, as Gallacher's account of it suggests.

As evictions began, Labour had, of course, to shift its priorities from the fight for the adoption of its own housing policies to the more immediate task of protecting tenants. Initially, they attempted this through pressure in council for representations to be made to the government on the urgency of rent control for the duration of the war. This was easily defeated, though there was noticeable support for the principle from outside the Labour group, reflected in the thirty-one votes cast for the Labour motion out of an attendance of over ninety in February 1915.

A month later, with tenants' associations forming rapidly

under formidable leaders like Jean Barbour in Govan, to resist the increases, Wheatley put a further Labour resolution to the council on rent control. He argued that almost all the houses whose rents were being raised had been built well before any relevant increases in interest rates and material costs had become the decisive factors claimed by owners: 'If it was unpatriotic for engineering workers to strike then it was also unpatriotic for property owners to strike against giving houses at rents that prevailed before the war.'[4] The principle of rent control was not, of course, likely to be adopted by the council at this stage, though the debate was valuable propaganda for Labour, and in the end the council settled for a predictably anodyne motion that Parliament merely be asked to inquire into the whole question of wartime rent increases. Glasgow Corporation's lack of urgency was paralleled by that of the government and persuaded some of Glasgow's more rapacious landlords to go for a further round of rent increases in areas like Govan, where effective resistance was certain from skilled workers and their wives.

The rent campaign became emotionally more highly charged when landlords began to give every indication of evicting the families of serving soldiers. A particularly arbitrary example of this involved Wheatley directly since it took place in his own Shettleston Council ward and, in fact, not far from where he himself and his family lived. The victim was the wife of Michael McHugh, a miner employed before the war in one of the several pits still being worked on the eastern fringes of Glasgow. McHugh had volunteered soon after the outbreak of war and had been badly wounded on the Western Front in the spring of 1915. His wife had five children to support out of her separation allowance. Two of these had caught whooping cough and pneumonia, and she fell into rent arrears, her rent having been increased from the end of April. Wheatley fought the McHugh case from the outset and, indeed, helped to make it a *cause célèbre* which threw the whole issue of wartime rental increases and evictions into a dramatic human focus. He accompanied Mrs McHugh to the Sheriff Court on the day that the factors had asked for the warrant of ejection to be granted. He wrote later of how they found themselves in a large ante-room to the burgh court with upwards of a hundred other women, mostly with children and many of them soldiers' wives. All were there to hear their fate pronounced by the local Sheriff who happened to be sitting that day. The bright and unfeeling chatter of a young well-dressed clerkess to the court grated on Wheatley for its apparent indifference to the misery of those who waited upon the court's decision.

Wheatley assumed that in Mrs McHugh's case a stay of eviction would be granted since her arrears were less than many others due to appear before or after her, while the miners' trade union, of which her husband had been a member, had undertaken to clear his family's arrears from its own funds. The Sheriff of the day, however, was unimpressed and ordered Mrs McHugh's eviction within forty-eight hours. 'Michael McHugh is defending his country against foreign invasion', Wheatley wrote after this, 'Shettleston must defend his family against the Huns at home.'[5] Feeling in Shettleston rose almost by the hour. A crowd of close to a thousand people, informed of the Sheriff Court verdict, gathered rapidly outside the tenement where the McHugh family lived and a Union Jack was nailed to the door giving access to it. Five hundred women went to the Shettleston constituency ILP rooms to offer their services on alternating picket duty outside the McHugh house, and when Wheatley spoke there on the evening of Wednesday, 16 June, close on 4,000 people were reckoned to be blocking the street itself. Over and above this, an angry march took place on the house of the factor who had initiated the eviction process. Missiles were hurled at the house, a police guard was mounted outside it, and the factor was ceremonially burned in effigy in the street outside. Wheatley did not endorse this particular manifestation of popular anger, having had a taste of it only three years before. When he reminded another protest meeting of this, his audience laughed it off and someone was heard to call, 'Never mind, John, you're aye here yet!⁶ Wheatley clearly hoped the agitation in his own ward would put pressure on the City Chambers in George Square, and at the next full council meeting, with the McHugh eviction still not carried out, he moved a Labour resolution for the suspension of Standing Orders. This was to clear the council's agenda for a vote on a further Labour motion that the council call upon the government to make illegal the eviction from their homes of serving soldiers' families. Wheatley's speech, closely argued as always, even managed to be conciliatory to the extent that he accepted, given the introduction of a rent freeze, that property owners should not have to meet the full cost of maintaining property which they had let. Public funds, he argued, could and should be drawn upon to assist them. This concession did nothing to protect him from the charge of blackguarding property owners and his motion was defeated by forty-six votes to thirty-four.

Wheatley combined his support for this particular tenant with a dramatic telegram, sent from the City Chambers, to Lord Kitchener urging action by the War Office against the eviction of soldiers' families. 'Numerous cases of absent soldiers' dependents here threatened with eviction for non-payment of rent', his telegram read. 'Appeal for and await your suggestions of protective measures.'⁷ The War Office's answer was wholly negative, merely advising Wheatley that existing separation allowances could not be increased to assist rental payments and that no action was, therefore, feasible by it as a department. Wheatley, of course, had not asked for an increase in separation allowances, so the War Office had really raised an irrelevant issue in their reply. This can best be seen as part of a strategy of evasion by them, since the Cabinet itself was still undecided on the rental question. The determined tactics used in Shettleston prevented the McHugh eviction from going ahead, but did not stop other landlords from seeking rent increases. Again they were resisted by marches, pickets and organised refusals to pay, Wheatley acting as a behind-the-scenes adviser to many of these tenants' associations and rent-strike committees. By October, with resistance solid and still growing, the government sought to buy time by instituting a two-man Committee of Inquiry, comprising a judge, Lord Hunter, and Professor W. R. Scott. When the committee held its first public sitting at the end of October, there was hardly a working-class locality in Glasgow not caught up in the strikes. Dollan estimated that 10,000 tenants were withholding their increases in Glasgow alone. Four of these were Labour councillors and by the month's end support was gathering momentum from well beyond the city, with supportive strike action threatened in the Lanarkshire coalfield.

Wheatley was among those called before the Hunter-Scott Committee to give evidence. In answer to cross-examination by Lord Hunter, he re-stated the case he had already made at a succession of meetings and in the press. High interest rates dictated by money-lenders and bond-holders were, he argued, the key to rent rises rather than any increase in building costs, since private enterprise had built so few new houses before the war. Owners must be encouraged to the full in any resistance they offered to the predatory demands of bond-holders, but equally must be prevented by law from using tenants as a way of paying for increased interest rates. Lord Hunter pressed Wheatley on the matter of wartime earnings, implying that in the munitions industry many workers could meet rent increases out of their increased pay. Many Shettleston men worked at the Beardmore Foundry at Parkhead or the Springfield Foundry near the Celtic football ground, and Wheatley, closely involved as he had been with the Clyde Workers' Committee, was well informed about wage rates and working conditions. Any increases they had gained from the war must, he reminded Lord Hunter, be seen in the context of heavy overtime and double shifts at weekends: 'When a man works seven days a week for about eight weeks he breaks down and loses a week or two for which he receives no wages. It is by this means that you may arrive at a fair estimate of an engineering worker's income.' All of Lord Hunter's questions were used by Wheatley to drive home his conviction that there was no equality of sacrifice in the war, and indeed that the real purposes of the war were far removed from those extolled by government propaganda. 'The worker bleeds and dies that property may prosper', he wrote in *Forward*, while the Hunter–Scott Inquiry was in session. 'Only the bodies and brains of the working class prevent the Kaiser and his friends from confiscating this island with its riches and its rents. Every sense or feeling that distinguishes man from the lowest animals would have prompted property owners to display gratitude and generosity to the workers in these circumstances had not the brutalising influence of the capitalist system banished the fine characteristics of the human race from dealings between rich and poor.'[8]

As important as Wheatley's evidence was that of civil servants attached to the Local Government Board in Scotland, who argued forcefully that private enterprise had provided virtually no new working-class housing for almost seven years and had no prospect of tackling any of the housing problems of Glasgow and the West of Scotland. By the time the committee reported to the cabinet on 3 November, it was clear that the strike movement was stronger than ever and wholly committed to rents being returned to their August 1914 level. Even so, the government still equivocated, torn between fear of large-scale industrial unrest developing from the rent question and aversion to any surrender to a militant working-class campaign.

Mackinnon-Wood, the Scottish Secretary, had acted indecisively in this crisis and the initiative for legislation came from Lloyd George, now Munitions Minister and with an eye on how best to calm unrest in an area as crucial to war industry as Clydeside. The government's answer was the Rent and Mortgage Interest Restriction Bill, which was rapidly enacted to hold rents for the rest of the War at their August 1914 level. Out of the co-operation locally between the Labour Party and the Women's Housing Association, a Scottish Labour Party Housing Association was formed in which Wheatley was active from the start, later becoming the chairman and doing as much as anyone to push its policy of interest-free local authority housing.

The 1915 rent strike was a significant working-class victory and as councillor, propagandist and adviser to people caught up in the struggle, Wheatley played his part. It was also a political education for him in the way that people, through disciplined agitation in their own localities, could gain some influence over their own destiny.

Running parallel to the rents campaign but outlasting it was another struggle based on the discontents of workers in the munitions industry. Defined loosely to cover all forms of war production, this by 1917 was employing some 250,000 workers in Scotland, most of them in the Glasgow area. The skilled core of this labour force had felt itself under attack before the war from employers who had absorbed American managerial theory and were pledged to production speed-ups, breaking union power and ending special rates for skilled male workers by the process of dilution, i.e. replacing them with the semi-skilled. In March 1915 the unions in the industry went some way, in the Treasury Agreements, to accepting deskilling and dilution, and controls over wartime industrial action. Militant shop stewards who opposed this formed the Clyde Workers Committee (CWC) and organised a series of strikes which brought to Glasgow in December 1915 Lloyd George, the Munitions Minister; then in January 1916 the government's three Dilution Commissioners whose remit was to secure local agreements over wartime controls over the industry as well as breaking the CWC.

The CWC's strategy had from the outset to be to force the commissioners to negotiate with it centrally over dilution. From the CWC's point of view the Beardmore Forge at Parkhead proved very soon to be the weak link in this strategy for reasons relating to its history as a plant with a distinct and proud sense of its own identity, to the ascendancy among its shop stewards of David Kirkwood and to Wheatley's personal influence over him. On 24 January 1916 the commissioners arrived at Parkhead and David Kirkwood agreed to meet them with the other stewards, and with Sir William Beardmore himself, that great patriarch of the Clydeside engineering industry, also present. Kirkwood's message to them was a clear declaration of his own willingness as a socialist to accept dilution provided that it was not going to be used as a cloak for the introduction of low-paid labour or for the erosion of hard-won union rights. It was only then that it became apparent to Kirkwood and the other stewards that the commissioners, in fact, had no plan of their own to serve as a basis for negotiation, and that their intention was to put the ball into the court of the Parkhead stewards.

Having promised the commissioners a Parkhead scheme

within twenty-four hours, Kirkwood was in no doubt what his next move would be: 'That night I went to John Wheatley. We collected shop-stewards from other works. Together we thrashed out the problem and John Wheatley began to write. In thirty minutes he had drafted the scheme.'[9] Wheatley, he recalled, had brought his mind to bear on the task in hand 'like a perfectly adjusted machine'.[10] The episode is illuminating evidence of the status Wheatley had by this time secured through patient self-education, and the resulting document shaped decisively the direction in which dilution policy would go.

The document began with a preamble accepting without reservation the need for war production to be increased. Perhaps this was a concession by Wheatley for negotiating purposes, but it reiterated that the stewards' only concern was to prevent patriotism being exploited as a way of bringing cheap labour into Clyde industry. The actual terms embraced an acceptance of the idea that the new dilutees' wages be based not on sex, previous training or experience, but on actual work completed and on the prevailing rate for particular operations. In this form, Wheatley's document could be interpreted as applying only to piece-workers and so went little beyond regulations already accepted by the government. On 2 February he and Kirkwood agreed to its amendment in such a way as to cover all 'dilutees', though this was accompanied by a declaration from the commission that the purpose of dilution was not to lessen labour costs but to increase output.

Dilutees would not, in fact, at once get the going rate under the Parkhead agreement; a time-lag, based on their need to acquire the necessary experience, was allowed for. Formal recognition of shop stewards' committees and workplace organisation was claimed by both Wheatley and Kirkwood as being integral to the agreement, though in fact Kirkwood was soon to find that he would have less than the full freedom he hoped for at Parkhead to check how the new system was working. Another loophole was the lack of any controls conceded to works committees over actual transfers of skilled workers to other plants arising from the rate at which dilution might be applied in Parkhead.

The Parkhead agreement was not, in fact, implemented for some weeks and was not publicised in the press for a fortnight. Gallacher only heard of it when he and his fellow members of the CWC came out of prison on bail on 8 February. From the point of view of the CWC, events at Parkhead were a betrayal by Kirkwood and Wheatley of any real hope of a common front of shop stewards in all plants likely to be affected by dilution. Its influence, indeed, as a body, survived from that moment only on borrowed time, not merely because Kirkwood and the Parkhead stewards had by-passed it, but because Lloyd George and the government were still biding their time before seeking to crush it.

There remains a problem, compounded by the lack of any of Wheatley's own papers and correspondence, about his motives in influencing the Parkhead agreement to the extent that he appears to have done. Arthur Marwick's view of him as the 'political genius'[11] in the background may exaggerate his role, though activists like Gallacher and Bell certainly thought that he wanted to cement an already developing influence over Kirkwood. Merely to claim, as does Middlemas,[12] that Wheatley's concern was to 'undo the extremists' means little, because other events had already involved him heavily with members of the CWC. Gallacher, John Muir and Walter Bell were arrested after an issue of the *Worker* produced by the committee had appeared on 29 January 1916 with an article entitled 'Should the Workers Arm'. The article argued against this proposition but even to discuss it exposed those involved in the paper's production to serious charges. The Dilution Commissioners, in fact, wanted everybody concerned arrested and deported out of Glasgow, but the Crown Office favoured trial by jury.

Wheatley, with Kirkwood, was Gallacher's first visitor after his arrest. Gallacher later recalled Wheatley's first concern being to get blankets for him since the prison authorities had not offered any. Here Wheatley had to admit defeat, for the warder with responsibility for Gallacher's cell could provide only lice-ridden ones. Gallacher, experiencing prison for the first time, found Wheatley's visit an enormous relief. So pleased was he that he later wrote that he would have agreed to almost anything that Wheatley proposed. Wheatley, in fact, confined himself to attending to the needs of Muir, whose morale went down quickly after his arrest, and engaging Rosslyn Mitchell, a socialist solicitor, to take charge of the three men's cases. Amidst protest strike action at several engineering and munitions plants, Gallacher, Muir and Bell were charged. Wheatley attended the court to see bail granted. Gallacher had hoped that Kirkwood might have thrown his weight behind sympathetic action at Beardmore's works. This did not happen, though Kirkwood attended the court with Wheatley to hear the charges, but his relationship with Wheatley was already a subordinate one in Gallacher's reckoning. 'From that time on', he later recalled, 'Wheatley's influence over several of the comrades became so pronounced that they would do nothing without consulting him.'[13] In Kirkwood's case, this influence (in Gallacher's view) confirmed his Parkhead sectionalism.

The trial of Gallacher, Muir and Bell took place at the High Court in 1918, following closely upon the conviction and sentencing there of John MacLean after his celebrated speech of defiance from the dock. Gallacher's trial, and that of Muir and Bell, were low-key affairs in comparison, though with an equally predictable outcome, despite Mitchell's attempts to persuade the defendants that they might get off with heavy fines. These proceedings diverted attention only temporarily from events in Glasgow developing out of the Parkhead agreement. The agreement, drafted by Wheatley and Kirkwood, soon became a basis for the CWC's own programme for submission to the Dilution Commissioners in mid-February. By that time, however, and in the aftermath of the Parkhead agreement, the commissioners had no real intention of dealing with the committee as a body or accepting its claims to represent twenty-nine yards and engineering shops on the Clyde. On 26 February, they formally refused demands for negotiations with the committee, and from that moment the question was really what issue would be used by the commissioners as a pretext for moving against the committee.

This was soon to be provided by the question of how the agreement should be interpreted. Kirkwood assumed that it guaranteed his freedom as shop stewards' convener to move around all sections of the works when, in fact, it did not. His role remained pivotal, given the tensions created by new labour brought in (especially to the new Howitzer shop) under the dilution scheme, and restrictions placed upon his movements in late February 1916 were in breach of the spirit of the agreement. More provocative still was the company's refusal in mid-March to recognise him any longer in his role as convener. Kirkwood, far from aiming at the subversion of war production, took pride in Parkhead's output and his part in maximising it, but this new move against him prompted immediate strike action in his support. Barely a week intervened between this and the arrest and deportation to Edinburgh in the early hours of 25 March of Kirkwood and eight other activists from Parkhead and Weirs of Cathcart. Kirkwood at least anticipated his arrest by taking the precaution of calling on Wheatley's Shettleston home to leave in his safe-keeping a bag with two hundred pounds of the CWC's funds in it.

Protest strikes elsewhere on the Clyde crumbled fairly quickly, and Wheatley, now responsible for the CWC's funds, made it his business to keep in contact with the deportees who, after their release were formally banned from the Glasgow munitions district but allowed to seek work outside the area in which their activities had made them conspicuous. They were treated leniently in fact, both by the Munitions Ministry and the military authorities at Edinburgh Castle who took some trouble to prevent the men from being black-listed outside Glasgow. Ten weeks later, Wheatley was able to assure readers of *Forward* that all the deportees had, in fact, found work, except for James Haggerty from Parkhead, who was still looking for a job, and Kirkwood.

Kirkwood was the best known of the deportees and was, indeed, victimised by hostile employers, despite unease over this in the Ministry of Munitions. He maintains, however, in his autobiography that he refused any offers of employment except back at Beardmore's Parkhead works, where he believed he had been unjustly treated and had the right to re-instatement. It has been implied that this was a result of Wheatley's influence and that he saw political advantage in converting Kirkwood into a proto-martyr and hero of the official Labour movement. This may well have been behind what looks very like Wheatley's stage-management of Kirkwood's appearance at the January 1917 Labour Conference in Manchester.

Wheatley attended the Manchester Conference, handled the arrangements for Kirkwood's journey to it, and conferred with him before his appearance. This caused great excitement amongst the delegates and was ostensibly to second one of his own union resolutions. In fact, he spoke eloquently in his own defence (possibly from notes prepared for him by Wheatley) and announced his defiant intention of returning to Glasgow in contravention of his deportation order from the Clyde munitions area. Wheatley accompanied him and continued to give him close support through a further period in which he was re-arrested, imprisoned in Edinburgh Castle and put under renewed pressure to accept his exclusion from Beardmore's, until Churchill, as Minister of Munitions, used his influence to get him work as a foreman, not at Parkhead but at another Beardmore plant, a shell factory in Mile End.

Wheatley, throughout this period, worked hard on behalf of all the deportees, as well as those like Gallacher and MacLean imprisoned for sedition. Nearly all had families who needed support, and Wheatley, as Treasurer of the Clyde Workers Defence and Maintenance Fund, had a central co-ordinating function in raising the funds needed. With MacLean, Wheatley's differences remained, but he was mindful of the wide sympathy in the labour movement for what he had suffered because of his opposition to the war.

Amidst all these other concerns, Wheatley's council work continued, assisted by a Labour group that increased as a result of contesting some seats vacated during the war. Chronic food shortages induced by the German U-boat campaign made for angry scenes in the council as Wheatley led the Labour group in a campaign against the well-stocked hotels in central Glasgow that seemed to him to mock the hardship in working-class areas. In response to the majority's indifference to their call for emergency action on food supply, Labour resorted to procedural obstruction and a protracted filibuster. Wheatley revealed an aptitude for these attritional tactics that won grudging admiration from the local press, which described him as

> the most persistent exponent of the gentle art of obstruction. His engaging amiability, his delightful urbanity were exhibited in a way which impressed more or less every auditor. What appeared to cheer him immeasurably in his labours – he must have spoken

about twenty-four columns of words – was the ebullient indignation of his hearers. Time and again points of order were raised and Mr Wheatley was requested to stick to the subject and not wander all over the earth. Such interruptions to the train of his thoughts he answered with honeyed words.[14]

There was more than a hint here of the formidable yet good-humoured presence which he would soon establish for himself at Westminster.

Wheatley was prepared, too, to act independently of the Labour group, an example being the council's decision to give Lloyd George, by then Prime Minister, the freedom of the city in late April 1917. He secured only five votes for his amendment to the proposal, after an angry speech in its support. Such an honour with the junketings which would accompany it, he declared, was an insult to a city that had lost thousands of men in the war, many of whose families were by 1917 living in near-famine conditions. Lloyd George, moreover, had a major share of the responsibility for deporting from Glasgow ten of its citizens without trial or the right to speak in their own defence. The Lloyd George visit seemed to Wheatley merely another device for glossing over the way those with wealth and property were cushioned from the worst hardships of the Home Front. 'No national sentiment for them', he declared, 'No patriotism. None of the beauty of sacrifice. These are the joys of the working class. The capitalists will be content with profit.'[15] He was also grimly amused by the altered emphasis of demographic debate about desirable family size. Imprudent working-class breeding had been forgotten by publicists preoccupied with Britain's loss of life in the war: 'Malthus has been hustled off the stage to make way for the war baby.'[16]

Perhaps Wheatley's most ill-judged foray against the war profiteers was a *Forward* article early in 1918 in which he seemed to be attributing working-class hardship to Jewish manipulation of interest rates. Addressing himself, as he sometimes did in his column, to a fictitious Michael Mulligan, an innocent and much put-upon Irish immigrant worker with a large family to support, he stressed the alleged role of Jewish finance in costing him and others like him as much 'to square the Jews'[17] as it did to defeat the Germans. The article brought angry protests and a prompt apology from Wheatley, who denied that he had been generalising about the Jewish community. He certainly had no record of anti-Semitism and was not subsequently ever accused of it. Indeed, it was just a few weeks later that, on a motion by Wheatley, Emanuel Shinwell was co-opted to the City Council to fill a vacancy caused by another member's death. Shinwell's Jewishness seems to have had no bearing, however, on the fact that their relationship was never a close one, personally or politically.

The campaign against the war itself continued, with Wheatley remaining active in its various rallies and meetings but also using the council to challenge the assumption that the war must be fought to a finish. He created uproar in November 1917 when, on behalf of the anti-war campaigner Helen Crawford, he tried to get a hearing for a Women's Peace Crusade deputation. His speech was shouted down and his motion lost, but if the labour movement could not halt the war or do much more than condemn conscription, it could at least put the case for the conscription of wealth acquired from the war. When the council's General Finance Committee sought authority to purchase £250,000 worth of War Bonds early in 1918, Wheatley led Labour's attack, arguing that fortunes already made from the war should be the target for appropriate levels of taxation which would contribute to the funding of the war's ever-mounting cost.

Wheatley had ceased to believe in the rationality of calling for a unilateral British withdrawal from the conflict, putting all his weight behind a negotiated peace and a European body with powers to arbitrate in all disputes between states. He returned to these themes at the May Day 1918 Rally on Glasgow Green, which as many as 70,000 people may have attended, not primarily because of John MacLean's release from prison (since the rally had been organised well before the announcement of his release), though that was also celebrated by many who were present.

Wheatley had been adopted as a parliamentary candidate for Camlachie in 1917, with the possibility of a general election following any conclusion to hostilities with Germany, but was looking for a better prospect than this constituency. In February 1918, he was given leave by the Glasgow Central Labour Party and the ILP's Glasgow Federation to accept adoption as prospective candidate for the new constituency of Shettleston. Some feathers were ruffled in Camlachie, where it was claimed that the proper procedures for releasing an adopted candidate had not been wholly fulfilled. Accusations, though unsubstantiated, were also made that Wheatley had communicated with the Shettleston selection committee while still Camlachie's prospective candidate. In all likelihood, what happened was that, living locally, he had signalled interest in the candidature on an informal basis without intending to breech procedural rules.

Labour in Scotland had, without a doubt, moved to the left in response to the war, something apparent in the resolutions of the party's Scottish Advisory Council at its conferences and of the ILP. Its Glasgow Federation in November 1917 adopted a militant manifesto rejecting 'patchwork' reforms and calling for full public ownership of industry with workers' control, restoration of the land to the people, free education for all and comprehensive housing programmes with interest-free rents.

Wheatley was not averse to most of this, but was beginning to bridle at an apparently growing addiction among some socialists to insurrection as a short-cut to power.

Events in Russia, of course, had given added impetus to those who saw a revolutionary road opening up in Britain. Wheatley, however, took a very guarded view of political stances and propagandist campaigns which aroused people without preparing them for the consequences. 'If we are out for revolution', he wrote, 'let us at least prepare to the extent of converting our bookstalls into munitions depots and our economics classes into rifle ranges.'[18] With the Coalition government committed to legislation which would double the working-class electorate, he could see socialism coming within the reach of constitutional political action. 'Granted political liberty and constitutional respect', he went on, 'I would regard a resort to violence as a terrible crime.'[19] His faith in 1918 was in political rather than industrial action, though events would soon test that faith, and Wheatley never saw the direct action of the war years as a purely temporary tactic in an abnormal situation.

The pre-conditions of day-to-day working-class existence, which good fortune and ability had given him an escape from, still preoccupied him. He declared in February 1918:

> To my mind, there is no more surprising spectacle in these rebel days than that of millions of men and women meekly leaving their homes, almost fasting on a cold winter's morning before six o'clock, dressed in dirty clothing and proceeding to workshops, shipyards and tramway depots of the most uninviting character, there to serve like dumb-driven cattle, having no voice in the arrangement of the starting hour, meal hours or stopping time, and usually without a say in the nature of their work, the manner of its performance, or the disposal of the product of their labour.[20]

It was to liberate and harness their energies and hopes that he looked ahead to the political campaigns of the post-war period

5 1918–1922: From council to Parliament

I

Labour in Scotland in December 1918 was ill-prepared for a general election and the unrest of the war years did not convert itself into electoral gains. From the outset of the campaign, conflicting views were voiced over Wheatley's prospects in Shettleston, but *Forward* was optimistic, praising his credentials for representing the constituency: 'He is a brilliant advocate. His handling of the housing question on the platform is a model of lucidity and carries conviction. He is an Irishman with all the keenness and vivacity that distinguishes the race:'[1] In his campaign Wheatley never strayed far from a Labour manifesto which laid emphasis on a peace of reconciliation, freedom for Ireland and India, Allied withdrawal from Russia, the land for the people, a capital levy and industrial democracy. This last theme fitted in well with speeches he had been making earlier in the year on the evils of 'Kaiserism' in industry, and the democratic management of production was a theme of several of his major speeches. He pressed for any government to accept trade union rates of maintenance for willing workers temporarily unemployed from the post-war dislocation of the labour market, and interest-free loans underwritten by government so that local authorities could begin to tackle the housing problem. 'My object,' he declared to one meeting a day or two before polling, 'is the elimination of landlordism, private profit, interest privilege, poverty, disease and ignorance from human society and the fostering of international brotherhood.'[2]

An important factor in the contest in Shettleston, and indeed in many other West of Scotland constituencies, was the voting intentions of Catholics of Irish descent. Until 1914, the United Irish League (UIL) in which Wheatley himself had once been so active, was the main outlet for political activists within the Catholic community whose first allegiance was still to the Irish national cause. The Easter Rising had posed some crucial questions about the future of constitutional Home Rule, while military service and population movement had drained the League's branches of much of their membership. On 30 November 1918, Charles Diamond, who since 1910 had become increasingly sceptical about the old Liberal–Irish nationalist alliance, urged in the columns of the paper he owned that Irish voters should now support Labour: 'We urge them to drop the policy of being, as it were, a foreign or floating factor in the body politic, giving their votes now on one side and now on the other, moved thereto by the question of Ireland, and so trusted by no party in the State.'[3]

The UIL, in fact, met for its annual conference before the general election with much of its organisation intact, for Sinn Fein had not made any advances in Britain comparable to its success in Ireland. Feeling for a Labour alliance certainly emerged in speeches from the floor. T. P. O'Connor, the League's veteran president and solitary MP, held the conference to the policy of no alliance with any one party and reiterated the case for supporting selected candidates deemed to be 'sound' on Irish Home Rule. Four weeks later the League executive sent out telegrams of support to twenty-six candidates in Scotland. Wheatley received one such telegram. He could hardly have been denied it given his support for Labour policy on Ireland and his patient work in seeking to convince the immigrant Irish that their political future lay with Labour.

Initially it seemed he would be standing in opposition to a Liberal as well as a Coalition Unionist. M. Boyd Auld was a weak candidate, however, and withdrew a clear three weeks before polling. This left the field clear for the works manager at the Parkhead Forge, Admiral Adair. The Admiral's campaign was colourful, using decorated floats on naval themes to dramatise the Coalition's patriotic credentials. He took a hard line on German reparations, and on the need for a government of strong men like Lloyd George and Bonar Law to confront the problems of peace. The uncertainties ahead demanded continued munitions and arms production to keep Britain strong, he declared in numerous speeches, another way of saying that a Coalition vote would help to maintain male employment in Shettleston.

The Coalition's commitment to full peacetime employment was a recurrent theme in his speeches, as was the need for skilled workers in the armed forces to be guaranteed their pre-war jobs upon demobilisation. The patriotic Labour Party of Clynes and Hodge could help in this work, unlike the 'red flag party' of Wheatley. The Admiral, however, could be caught out with questions, as ILP supporters discovered. At one meeting it was recorded that under pressure from the floor he referred a question to another heckler who might supply him with an answer. For Wheatley, his initiation into parliamentary elections was an experience that he gave every indication of enjoying, and admiral Adair's campaign was a clean one compared to what he would later have to confront.

The real shadow cast over the contest was provided by Manus, or 'Mandy' M'Gettigan, Wheatley's former business associate with whom his partnership had just been dissolved. M'Gettigan, in his resentment over the way this had been done, circulated various statements and allegations about

Wheatley's business affairs when the Shettleston contest started. Wheatley had already initiated a legal action for £2,000 damages for slander, and also to secure an interdict to stop M'Gettigan's interventions in the campaign. These had included the circulation of statements purporting to be from Wheatley about his finances. The threat of legal action compelled M'Gettigan to admit that these were forgeries and he accepted Wheatley's condition that he write a full admission for *Forward* of the methods by which he had furthered his quarrel with him.

Wheatley took part in the culmination of Labour's Glasgow campaign, an emotional rally in St Andrews Hall on the eve of polling. Many failed to gain admission to the meeting at which MacDonald made an eloquent speech, addressing himself amidst cheers to uniformed soldiers in the audience in order to make the point that democratic statesmanship could have ended the war sooner and on better terms. His peroration commended to his hearers Labour's message as 'a gospel of hope and a banner of revolt'.[4] His audience then joined the growing crowd outside for a march to George Square. In *Forward*'s words, 'Sauchiehall Street was taken by storm as the march moved off at 10 pm with a gigantic red standard at its head.'[5]

The Scottish press overestimated Labour's likely gains, the *Glasgow Herald* reckoning that in Glasgow alone it might take five seats. Of its Glasgow candidates only Neil MacLean won in Govan by a majority of 815. In Scotland as a whole six seats were won, while Barnes held Gorbals on the 'Coalition Labour' ticket. Wheatley's result in Shettleston turned out to be the most marginal in Scotland, Admiral Adair winning the seat for the Coalition with a majority of only seventy-four. The poll of 62.7 per cent was a little higher than that in Glasgow as a whole, but there were major problems in registering all those entitled to vote, especially those still in the armed forces. 'So much had been expected and so little gained', declared a *Forward* article after the results were known, but it applauded Wheatley for coming so close to victory, and pointed out to readers that Labour's overall vote of 323,000 in Scotland would have seemed inconceivable in 1914. In Britain as a whole, Labour polled 2 million votes without, of course, any reliance on the electoral pact with the Liberals which had been operative at the previous three general elections.

Renewed industrial unrest in Glasgow quickly followed the 1918 election. and Wheatley remained closely in touch with Kirkwood, Muir and Gallacher in the sequence of events culminating in the engineering workers' strike of January 1919 and Glasgow's celebrated 'Red Friday' on 31 January. He had no trade union base of his own from which to influence events, and there is evidence of a very distinct cooling in relations between him and Gallacher, who had already been dubious about Wheatley's influence over Kirkwood and about his intervention in the crisis of 1916. Wheatley, moreover, had been increasingly critical about the strike as a political weapon in his *Forward* articles earlier in the year.

The engineers' strike developed out of a series of decisions by the Scottish Trades Union Congress (STUC), the Amalgamated Society of Engineers (ASE) and the Glasgow Trades Council to mount a major challenge to employers on the Clyde and elsewhere. Their objective was to limit working hours and protect jobs in an industry where fear of the consequences of the end of war contracts was widespread. The background to the strike was confused, involving conflicting demands as to what a reduced maximum working week should be. The ASE's Glasgow District Committee was more militant in its demands than the national union leadership and was supported by a revived Clyde Workers Committee. The ASE, in fact, suspended its own Glasgow District Committee for departing from a

recommendation that a forty-seven-hour maximum be demanded, though the strike has gone down in history as the forty-
hour strike. Technically, it was unofficial action with patchy
support from other workers, despite heavy picketing to bring
out Glasgow electricity power workers. The belief that they
would support the strike was, indeed, one reason for the cabinet in London agreeing to the dramatic reinforcement of
troops already in the city.

The failure of the strike made Wheatley increasingly critical
of industrial action conceived of as an alternative to political
agitation and election campaigns. He was dubious about the
tactics used to launch the strike, and of the decision by the
ASE District Committee and the Trades Council to persuade
the Lord Provost of Glasgow that he should communicate their
demands to the government in the form of a telegram.
Wheatley, on his own admission a little later, had been ready
to believe that the Lord Provost had 'acted out of a high sense
of fair play', and the *Glasgow Herald* certainly denounced the
idea of the municipality of Glasgow becoming any sort of
mediator between the strikers and the state. However, once it
became clear that the Lord Provost's telegram to Downing
Street had been worded in such a way as not merely to
express the strikers' demands but to impress upon the government the need for intervention to break the strike, Wheatley
joined fiercely in attacks in the Council Chamber on the way
the District Committee and Trades Council had been deceived.

The climax of the strike was the rally in George Square on
Friday 31 January in support of a deputation which was to
receive a reply at the City Chambers from the Lord Provost
about the results of his approach to the government. The size
of the rally, at a point when some 70,000 workers had joined
the strike, and the ferocity of police measures to clear the
square, quickly overshadowed this. The indiscriminate police

77

baton charges in a packed square have often been described and have given the events of that day a legendary place in Scottish Labour history. Wheatley observed events from inside the City Chambers where his duties as councillor had taken him as the demonstration began to gather outside, but he was at Kirkwood's side when he was carried into the building unconscious and bleeding from the beating he had taken from police in the square.

He was also Gallacher's first visitor in the police cells after his arrest for his part in the day's events. He took with him the lawyer Rosslyn Mitchell in order to reassure Gallacher that his legal defence would be taken care of. Gallacher was contemptuous of the offer, informing both of them that he would conduct his own defence and later wrote dismissively of Mitchell in his account of these events. Despite this rebuff, Wheatley visited Gallacher again in Duke Street prison the night before he was due to stand trial in Edinburgh. Gallacher recalled that Wheatley was confident that he, Gallacher, could cope with another sentence, but fearful of what effect a further spell in prison might have on his protégé, Kirkwood. He need not have worried, for the jury acquitted Kirkwood. Wheatley went to Edinburgh for the trial, accompanying Gallacher's wife and sitting with her to hear her husband get a three-month sentence. His next appearance in Parliament House would be not as a spectator, but as the central figure in a major legal drama. By the time the Edinburgh trials started, the strike was long since over, ended by its own weaknesses and by a military presence in and around Glasgow which, though not used, may certainly have halted the heavy picketing that would have been needed to widen support for the engineering workers.

Events more turbulent and violent than anything that had happened in Glasgow were reshaping Irish history in the post-war period. In 1918, like the labour movement as a whole, Wheatley had been slow to comprehend what the Easter 1916 Rising signified, but he condemned the executions which followed it, though continuing to distance himself from a middle-class Sinn Fein nationalism which he deemed to be extraneous to real working-class issues.

The executions, of course, changed everything, as the columns of the *Glasgow Observer* remind us, and once the war's end brought both a decisive Sinn Fein election victory and guerrilla insurgency over much of Ireland, Wheatley joined the campaign for British withdrawal and an end to the excesses of Crown forces employed against the rebellion. He was a leading speaker at the 1919 May Day Rally on Glasgow Green, along with Countess Markiewicz, when Irish tricolours were carried openly among a crowd of 100,000 and the 'Soldier's Song' was sung, as well as 'The Red Flag'. Later that year he spoke again at a 'hands off Ireland' meeting which filled St Andrews Hall with 5,000 people, leaving another 5,000 outside.

When a settlement on the basis of the partition of Ireland became imminent, he held to the unyielding position he had taken almost ten years before in the crisis unleashed by the Liberal government's Home Rule Bill. He did not flinch from attacking *Forward* over its views favouring partition, which to him was a betrayal of Labour's policy of no coercion and no partition.

The year 1919 and the early months of 1920 were an encouraging time for those on the Labour left. In January of 1920 the Scottish Divisional Council of the ILP voted for affiliation to the new Third International, which Lenin had founded in Moscow, though a motion for the ILP to disaffiliate from Labour was defeated. Wheatley used his growing influence to rally opinion behind a parliamentary and electoral strategy as the movement's most important priority, and warned in a series of articles against diversions from it. More strike action, he insisted, could win only palliatives at high cost: 'The policy of industrial action only meant peaceful starvation as a means of winning Socialism or reliance on force. It assumed that people who did not want Socialism would starve or die for it. If they did want it, there is no need to do either.'[6]

If the strike and the insurrection that had brought the Soviet state into being offered, in Wheatley's view, no lessons for British socialists, he did identify himself strongly with that state in the summer of 1920 when its survival, and indeed the peace of Europe, seemed threatened by the hostility to it of Britain and France. He spoke in support of many resolutions of the Glasgow ILP's Executive Council, calling for British withdrawal from involvement in the brutal civil war waged against the Bolsheviks by their enemies within Russia. This campaign culminated in the formation in many places of Councils of Action in August to resist what seemed imminent intervention by Britain in support of the reconstituted Polish state in its war with the USSR. Hostility to the Coalition government's policy went well beyond Labour and the unions, a fact which contributed to the success of the 'Hands Off Russia' movement. Wheatley played his part in an agitation which was particularly well-organised and vocal in Glasgow, and was a leading speaker at the biggest rally held in the city.

Wheatley drove himself fiercely in these months, for the business affairs of Hoxton and Walsh ate into time he needed for a growing workload on the council. He chaired, during 1919, a special committee which Labour had pushed for to raise government support for employment schemes in the city and he was involved in much lobbying of the Ministry of Labour's Scottish Department. He was quick also to re-launch his pre-war housing strategy as a means not merely of providing for the homeless, but as a source of jobs in a depressed building industry. A resolution by him to secure a council pledge to build 1,500 houses with, or without, the consent of central government failed in May 1819, but not before he managed to secure a hearing by the full council of a deputation from the Women's Section of the Glasgow Labour Party Housing Association. This same year saw his influence on the council grow as he became chairman of the Works Committee and also of the Agricultural Produce Committee. To these responsibilities were added in the following year the joint convenership of the Housing and General Town Improvement Committee, another position from which Labour could direct its fire on the complacency over unemployment, not just of the council majority but of the Coalition government. Hard upon this appointment came the chairmanship of a Committee on Allowances to Dependents of Soldiers and Sailors, and his elevation to the bench of magistrates.

Actual contact with the political leaders of the day could be a by-product of council work, and early in 1920 Wheatley attended a housing conference convened by Lloyd George at 10 Downing Street. He was a member of a Glasgow deputation which found itself, with others from areas with problems as acute, listening to a lengthy address by the Prime Minister which singled out the restrictive practices of the building unions as the major problem and rejected all the deputation's recommendations. Wheatley did at least get a hearing for his advocacy of a municipal banking experiment to ease the cash-flow problems of local authorities anxious to build. Labour councillors were very clear that they had got nowhere with Lloyd George and their anger was still simmering a week later when rents and housing were debated in Glasgow's City Chambers. Wild scenes led to business being suspended with Wheatley seeking to have the Lord Provost evicted from the civic chair because of his unfitness to preside over council business.

Glasgow's unsolved housing problem had become acute

since the end of the war, and this seemed to some to draw Wheatley quickly into a course of action that called in question the parliamentarism he had been urging on the Labour movement since before the defeat of the 1919 engineering workers strike. His passionate involvement in housing questions before and since the 1915 rent strike made it impossible for him not to be drawn into renewed agitation precipitated by government policy, and by Glasgow's property owners' and house factors' assumption that an end to war in Europe would mean a renewed rent war in Glasgow, even though an Act of 1919 prolonged the wartime freeze on rent increases into 1921.

When the Ballantyne Royal Commission on Housing in Scotland finally reported, its conclusions, and the evidence upon which they were based, gave Wheatley the ammunition he needed to renew his campaign on the housing issue, and in August 1919 he had urged upon the council, quoting at length from the commission's findings, that the commercial market as a means of funding essential house-building had reached the end of the road. The commission had, indeed, found as a majority in favour of the view that 'the State, in assuming full responsibility for housing, should operate through the Local Authorities and should place upon them the responsibility of seeing to the provision of housing'.[7]

The sharp rise in building costs since 1914 was the industry's excuse for the virtual cessation of house-building in Glasgow, and Scotland as a whole, while the Coalition, despite the brief promise of Christopher Addison's housing legislation in 1919, was clearly not disposed to put any pressure either on the industry or on the local authorities. Rent increases, based either on loopholes in the 1915 Act or on amending legislation, were widely assumed to be imminent, and at its conference in August 1919 the Scottish Labour Housing Association (SLHA) came under strong pressure from some delegates for a ballot on a rent strike. This was defeated, partly because the Coalition's legislative intentions had not fully taken shape. The association had another special meeting in January 1920 at which Wheatley, from the chair, impressed upon the 4,000 delegates the growing urgency of the problem with 4,000 families registered on council waiting lists, many of them homeless, and reminded them of how many more garages for private cars had been built in Glasgow than had houses since the end of the war.

By early 1920 the government's commitment to a radical modification of the system of rent control introduced in 1915 was becoming clear. This took the form of a bill to enable landlords to apply 15 per cent increases on net rental, as well as an additional 25 per cent where the landlord was responsible for all the repairs. This latter provision covered virtually all working-class housing in Glasgow and, in May, Wheatley issued his first call for a no-rent campaign to the Labour Housing Association, declaring that the owners' entitlement to more rent for houses built long before the war was no greater than a claim for further payment from the men who had built them.

Wheatley himself did not at this point own his house in Shettleston, having only a lease on it from its owner, a local man called Falconer. In the course of the no-rent struggle Falconer terminated Wheatley's lease, and the family had to move to smaller premises in nearby Hill Street. Falconer was a local Conservative and Wheatley, on occasions, referred to his own impending eviction, but the reasons for it do not appear to have been political. In any case, his secure income enabled Wheatley to find an alternative house quickly, though he did not buy his own home until 1925.

His own circumstances had little bearing, in fact, on the campaign against the 1920 Act. Though he had recently been putting up a reasoned defence of Labour's commitment to take power through elections and through Parliament, Wheatley associated himself from the outset with militant action to render inoperative a statute for which he felt the Coalition had no democratic mandate. In a pamphlet which he wrote against the 1920 Act, he set out the issue as he saw it in terms wholly calculated to justify refusal of rent increases:

> The voice of the people is the voice of Parliament and however much we may hate a law we must obey that law because it expresses the will of the people. But what is our duty if a law is made – not only without popular sanction – but in direct violation of the conditions on which its members were sent to Parliament? Surely we owe no allegiance whatever or respect to Members of Parliament as individuals divested of their representative capacity? When they exceed their authority derived from the people they have no authority.[8]

For a time the no-rent campaign seemed to be mobilising massive support. The STUC called a special conference to pledge its backing through rallies and strike action, while local ILP branches co-operated actively with rent-strike committees and, indeed, sometimes became the nucleus of such committees. 'In this fight we cannot fail', Wheatley declared, 'Not a single family will be evicted. Any attempt to arrest wages can be answered immediately by a general strike.'[9] He was among the speakers at an enormous no-rent rally in Glasgow Green at the end of August, which was perhaps the climactic point of a real bid by Labour on the Clyde to by-pass the Parliamentary Party through a local alliance with unions and tenants' associations to thwart the Coalition's strategy.

The campaign had inherent weaknesses, however. There had been disagreement from the start over whether to refuse merely to pay the increases under the 1920 Act or to refuse any rents until the increases were abandoned. This was apparent at meetings both of the SLHA and the STUC, and the promised industrial action proved to be limited in scope. Actual support from tenants was uneven; the pages of *Forward* demonstrate this. By September, Andrew McBride, Wheatley's deputy in the SLHA, was expressing doubt as to whether the poorer localities could sustain the struggle. Much of its strength lay in Govan, Kingston and especially Clydebank amongst skilled shipyard and engineering workers, in stark comparison to the city's East End and to even patchier support further afield.

The STUC concluded that the rent strike had failed because the 'extraordinary scarcity of housing accommodation seemed to be too great for the maintenance of solidarity, the people being too much afraid of being rendered homeless to continue their resistance for any length of time'. [10] Wheatley, at the forefront though he had been, was not the man to blame those less comfortably circumstanced than himself for not having been able to see the fight through, and channelled his energy on housing matters back into his council work and the preparation of a longer term Labour strategy that would be the basis of legislation permanently associated with his name after 1924. Nevertheless, the housing question would re-surface in such a way as to be of material help to Wheatley and Labour as a whole in the next general election, and the strike did produce an important sequence of Sheriff Court judgements ruling against rent increases under the 1920 Act.

Beyond the temporary momentum achieved by the campaigns against rent increases and British intervention in the USSR Labour had set its sights on becoming a decisive force in local government. An opportunity to do this in Glasgow was provided by ward boundary changes under which all the city's increased number of council seats were to be contested in 1920. Ostensible 'non-party' ratepayers' groups, like the Good Government Committee, fought hard to prevent the Empire's 'second city' going socialist, and did not hesitate to attack

Labour's Catholic and Irish connections. Only twelve of Labour's eighty candidates had entered politics, like Wheatley, through the United Irish League, and scare-mongering against them to mobilise an Orange vote was a dubious tactic. The League's role as the standard-bearer of constitutional Irish nationalism in Scotland had become redundant since the 1916 Easter Rebellion in Dublin and a secure Labour–Irish alliance was already in the making, as elections to the new education authorities, created under the 1918 Education (Scotland) Act, had shown.

The 1920 council elections gave Labour a huge injection of optimism, for out of 111 Glasgow seats forty-four fell to Labour in a 79 per cent poll. Wheatley easily held his Shettleston seat and was joined on the council by his protégé Kirkwood, who was elected to fill the second Shettleston seat created by municipal boundary alterations. Wheatley already had a seniority within the Labour group on the council which had given him the status of an unofficial leader for several years, but after the election his position was formalised and he became Labour group chairman.

This contest for control of the enlarged city council was overlaid by a city-wide poll in 1920 under the terms of 1913 legislation to determine whether voters wanted a reduction in licences to sell drink, no licences at all or a simple adherence to the status quo. Twenty-four of the city's thirty-seven wards produced a clear verdict in favour of the status quo. Labour, like the STUC, had voted earlier for prohibition at its 1920 Scottish Conference and so was vulnerable to attack from temperance opinion because of the Irish publican influence alleged to be infiltrating its membership with the breakup of the old United Irish League. Wheatley, himself an abstainer, was not directly attacked, though his business, Hoxton and Walsh, had connections through its shareholders with the licensed trade.

The time was not far off when these would be used as part of a damaging vendetta against him by his opponents in Glasgow.

In the City Council a Labour majority was still in the future, but a much strengthened party group could make more impact on council business. Sometimes this was done in ways that imposed a strain upon Wheatley's position as Labour group chairman in the City Chambers. Calculated disorder in the chamber and challenges to the Lord Provost's rulings became a frequent occurrence in 1921 and 1922 as the hard reality of post-war unemployment began to make Labour councillors increasingly ready for calculated acts of disruption that were to become associated before long in the public mind with the Clydeside group of MPs in Westminster.

Early in 1920 the council was plunged into uproar when Labour opposed the Freedom of Glasgow being granted to the Prince of Wales. Although the relevant committee minute sanctioning this was approved, the chaos created by Labour opposition spilt out from the benches to the floor itself, leading to the knocking over of the Lord Provost's mace. A locally initiated scheme to provide free milk from the council's Health Department for nursing mothers and children under five caused further acrimony over Labour allegations that Standing Orders were being used to delay the implementation of the scheme. Dollan led Labour in this clash and accused opponents by name of personal responsibility for the likely deaths of children in Glasgow.

Wheatley on occasions led the attack for Labour, though often with an eye to actual victories, however limited, which might be won when doubters and waverers among the moderate majority could be swayed into voting with Labour. A local fund to assist the unemployed with rent arrears was created in this way; the actual fund was small but a principle at least was recognised. However, Wheatley could get as angry as any of his Labour colleagues about the complacency of the majority. In one debate on a report by the council's Committee on Unemployment he shouted across the chamber that 'if the women and weans of some of those present were starving it was not very difficult to imagine that they would very soon let the city and the people know what were the rights of human beings.'[11] Frequently, of course, he found himself having to answer the charge that the scenes that Labour councillors were involved in were a positive incitement to disorder among the unemployed. Labour's role as a voice for them in the council and in Parliament, he would often answer, could, in fact, reduce the risk of real street violence. 'The Labour Party', he told hecklers of one of his council speeches, 'the members of which are meeting many of those unemployed persons constantly, have done you a very great service in that connection.'[12] Control of a large elected local authority like Glasgow was always in his view a worthwhile socialist aim, in keeping with what he had written earlier of the key role that anti-statist decentralised municipalism would have in any socialist future.

This made him glad to see Labour infiltrating major council committees and securing many of the most important chairs and convenerships which did, indeed, happen after the major gains of the 1920 council elections. Yet, as Labour group chairman, he clearly felt bound to take a flexible view over the way his younger colleagues were ready to defy stuffy council conventions and disrupt business. Discipline within the group was not always easy. Shinwell and Tom Kerr (who later became a Labour Lord Provost himself) actually resigned from the Labour council group in 1920 after a debate on party discipline.

On this occasion a motion was tabled that there should be no defiance of the Lord Provost's rulings or disruption of procedure by Labour councillors unless a party group meeting had so decided. Kerr described this as requiring him and his colleagues to give the group twenty-four hours' notice of losing their tempers. This motion was not accepted, in fact, and Wheatley from the chair was left to reiterate the principle of group discipline. His ten years on the council reveal him as no respecter of mere convention for its own sake, but as an increasingly able manipulator of procedure and committee work on behalf of the people he represented and in order to make well-publicised socialist propaganda. In this sense his time in the City Chambers was an important preparation for the grander stage of Westminster.

II

The breakup of the Lloyd George Coalition in 1922 forced upon Labour another general election which, in Scotland, it was as ill-prepared for as it had been in 1918. A short-lived post-war boom had been followed by rapidly increasing unemployment which caused a haemorrhage of active party members who ceased to be able to keep up either their activism or their financial support. Only ninety-eight of the ILP's 231 Scottish branches were able to be represented at the 1921 Scottish Divisional Conference, and a year later the figure fell to sixty-seven. The party's Scottish reports in these years accepted unemployment as a self evident cause of lost membership.

In the Shettleston constituency which Wheatley was to contest again, ILP organisation and the willingness of volunteer workers were enough to compensate for any shortage of cash resulting from loss of members. This allowed Wheatley to campaign outside the bounds of his own constituency. He chaired a major rally of all Labour candidates in the West of Scotland and in his address mocked the Liberal–Tory contest which had taken over from the Coalition's breakup, comparing it to a fraudulent boxing match in which the spoils would be amicably divided after a token battle.

Wheatley's organising and polemical skills certainly pushed him to the centre of Labour's campaign in the West of Scotland, and John Scanlon recalled the contest as one in which 'the official programme issued by the Labour Party was largely ignored, and the election fought on a series of leaflets and manifestos drafted mainly by Wheatley'.[13] Fund-raising was the major problem, and in Glasgow the ILP picked up most of the bills, financing ten of Labour's twelve contests in the city.

In a well-orchestrated contest, Wheatley's victory was never much in doubt. That was certainly Dollan's view in the extended coverage he gave the elections and the preparations for them in *Forward*. Wheatley himself knew the constituency well enough to write off its eastern periphery which had retained something of its earlier village quality with a middle-class electorate which sat 'resentfully in its comfortable homes glowering at the invading proletariat who have sprung up.'[14] Votes lost there, his agent Robert Baxter believed, could easily be cancelled out by the organisation built up over a period of years for local council contests and for the 1918 general election.

Baxter, indeed, seems to have been any candidate's dream, with his minute knowledge of the constituency and the flawless skill with which he organised canvassing before the election and the mobilisation of the vote on the day itself. With half an hour until the polls closed, he reckoned that less than fifty Wheatley supporters recorded in canvasses had not voted, 'and they were being sought out'.[15] Organisation like this was a product of the availability of what Wheatley himself guessed was close to a thousand campaign workers. Strikingly too, for a Labour contest, Baxter had secured the aid of twenty motorists with their vehicles who ferried voters to the polls round the clock, covering 940 miles on their day's journeys.

Organisation of this quality had as its end result the communication of a message that had meaning for the daily lives of Shettleston people. Wheatley wrote:

> we talked local politics, advocating the claims of the Far East of Glasgow rather than those of the Near East of Europe. . . We won because we had saturated the Division with socialist propaganda, because we fought to win at every municipal election, and because a splendid force of common men and women rallied to the colours, submerged selfishness and worked without rest until victory was secured.[16]

Throughout Britain Labour won 142 seats, twenty-nine of them in Scotland as a whole and ten of these in Glasgow. The 32.5 per cent of the Scottish vote was more than Labour raised south of the border, a pattern, in fact, to be maintained at every subsequent general election until 1935. It needs to be recalled that only forty-three of the Scottish seats were contested and fourteen of those had not been fought by Labour in 1918 either. Nine, moreover, of the twenty-nine seats won went to Labour on a minority of the vote cast.

Some important ground has now been broken in analysing the importance of the swing to Labour in Clydeside and Glasgow proper between 1918 and 1922. By-elections, apart from Bothwell, are absent as a pointer to the 1922 result, but Labour's gains in the 1920 local elections were striking, with its vote topping the 80 per cent mark in wards within the very constituencies where it would do best two years later in the general election. Wheatley's own base in Shettleston was a very clear example of this. In the council elections of 1921 and 1922, the latter taking place only ten days before the parliamentary contest, Labour's gains were less dramatic but sufficient to consolidate the ground captured in the great breakthrough into the enlarged municipality in 1920.

If there was a single issue that worked to Labour's advantage it was certainly housing. The post-war threat, with the

Coalition's connivance, to the protection of tenants enshrined in the Act achieved by the 1915 rent strike, was skilfully exploited in Labour's propaganda. Wheatley had long since identified the pre-eminence of the housing issue and, before the 1922 elections, the law courts served to maximise its impact. 'It is seldom that the pieces on the board are arranged in a favourable setting for Labour',[17] Wheatley wrote after the election results were known, and he was referring here to the test case of *Kerr* v. *Pryde*, brought to court with Kirkwood's assistance by the Clydebank branch of the Labour Housing Association. Essentially, this case centred upon a legal debate over the meaning of the law as it related to notice of rent increases. The association's case was that any tenant must have notice to quit before a rent increase could legally be imposed upon him. A parallel English court case produced a verdict favourable to the association's view, and both the Court of Session in Edinburgh, then the House of Lords on appeal endorsed this. This last development came on 3 November 1922, rousing the *Glasgow Herald* to fury at the prospect of every tenant of a working-class house being given an entitlement to retrieve, as a result of rent increases over the last year, a sum equivalent to nearly twelve months' rent and rates combined.

Wheatley, with Kirkwood's assistance, was prompt in producing a manifesto in the name of the SLHA warning all tenants of the danger of Liberals or Tories, whether returned to office separately or in a new Coalition, taking immediate legislative steps to reverse the recent court decision. With their ears to the ground in their own areas, they were able to warn *Forward* readers that 'the owners have already asked the government to pass legislation authorizing them to retain the money illegally collected'.

Many of Wheatley's own most committed constituency supporters who had worked for his victory had graduated to political activism in the 1915 and 1920 rent agitations and he was in no doubt as to what the issue meant to them. 'The question of overpaid rent', he wrote after the election, 'is not a triviality, it symbolises the great struggle between property and the property-less. This cleavage was kept prominently before the electors from start to finish and there will be no moderating of the feud.'[18]

The factor working to Labour's advantage in Scotland in 1922 and already touched upon earlier, was the transfer to it of so much of the Catholic and Irish vote. T. P. O'Connor, grand old man of constitutional Irish nationalism in Britain and the old Home Rule Party's solitary MP for a mainland British constituency, put his failing strength behind one last attempt to hold the Irish vote together. *The Times* took special notice of his attempt to do this in Glasgow and the West of Scotland. Its correspondent, who set off from London rather in the manner of an explorer heading into the uncharted African interior, in fact based a good deal of his analysis upon an interview which Wheatley gave him. 'There is nothing in British socialism', Wheatley told *The Times*, 'that is directed against the Church. The two can live separately. One result has been that since we [i.e. the Catholic-Irish in Scotland] came into the movement, Socialist attacks on the Church have practically ceased all round and there has been a marked diminution of the old sectarian feeling.'[19] He may have been right in thinking that sectarianism within the labour movement was on the wane, but as the increasingly public figure he now became, he would have occasion to learn that opponents would not scruple to use his own background and religion as weapons against him.

The explosion of joy which greeted the 1922 election results in Glasgow and the euphoria with which its new MPs, with others like Shinwell and Tom Johnston, were seen off to Westminster on the night of Sunday, 19 November 1922 have often been described. After a day of emotional rallies and a solemn service of dedication in St Andrew's Hall, huge crowds jammed St Enoch's Station and the streets leading to it in expectation of the new MP's arrival for their train. No scene like it has been repeated in Glasgow or any British city since. Shinwell, writing many years later, could still recall 'as a memorable, terrifying experience' his struggle to reach the waiting train. The crowd all around him with its almost frightening passion and expectation seemed to him to be full of 'eyes which once again had the gleam of hope where despair had too long held sway'.[20] Wheatley was there, too, as a swelling chorus of the 'Internationale' rose from the packed crowd and red banners were held aloft.

One shrewd observer of the labour movement at this time, John Paton, saw in Wheatley a man deeply affected by the 1922 election, and one whose posture in parliament quickly became more uncompromising and militant than it had been in the days of his patient work in Shettleston and Glasgow City Chambers on local issues. The clue to this change came, in Paton's recollection, in a conversation they had during a train journey some while after the election. He noted the substance of his conversation at the time and his later publication of it is worth quoting. Wheatley agreed with Paton that the public expression of his views had taken on a sharper cutting edge since entering Parliament but denied that the quality of his socialism had altered merely to suit a national stage. He accepted, however, that in council politics he had always been guided by an aversion to maximum programmes, worth little until real support for them had been carefully built up. He had been convinced that public opinion was not ready for large-scale socialist proposals and had shaped his policies accordingly. Paton recalled Wheatley going on to say:

But the election has changed all that and proved to me that I was wrong. When I saw, on that Sunday night after the election, when we left Glasgow for London, the streets lined with hundreds of thousands of people cheering the new MP's, when I saw the square in front of the station jammed tight with over a hundred thousand citizens madly enthusiastic, not for the MPs themselves but the Socialism for which they stood, it was proved to me beyond doubt that the people were ready to respond to a bold Socialist lead.[21]

To help provide that lead, however, he was leaving a secure base in the municipality of Scotland's largest city for the political capital of and Anglo-British state which could impose its will both on Glasgow and on Scotland itself.

6 Parliament 1922–23

Wheatley, it has been suggested in David Marquand's life of MacDonald, was considered by Maxton as a suitable nominee for the leadership in 1922 of the greatly enlarged Parliamentary Labour group created by the election. Other accounts challenge this and, had it been true, it would have been a serious misjudgement by Maxton since Wheatley was not yet well known outside Scotland. Maxton may have voted against MacDonald at a private meeting of ILP MPs in Johnston's Court off Fleet Street on 20 November, but the next day, when the full Parliamentary Party assembled, there was certainly no nomination of Wheatley who was on record already for his support of MacDonald. Maxton voted with the Clydeside group to guarantee their compatriot his majority over Clynes, a less than magnetic figure during his two years as leader. 'We were Ramsay MacDonald's men. It was the Clyde group of Labour members who made Ramsay MacDonald the leader of the Party',[1] Kirkwood later wrote with more than a degree of exaggeration. John Scanlon, who for a time worked closely with Wheatley as his secretary, had lobbied on MacDonald's behalf, and later quoted Arthur Henderson's prediction that the Clyde group would be at odds with MacDonald in six months. The prediction was wrong only in that the honeymoon period lasted barely half that time.

Wheatley took quickly enough to the procedure of the

Commons, but he soon showed that he was no more prepared to be slavishly bound by rules than he had been as a councillor in Glasgow. He wasted little time in making his maiden speech, choosing the debate on the Address from the throne to open the new session. The debate ranged generally over economic policy, and Wheatley was called after Lady Astor had withstood some heckling from the Labour benches which had prompted her to lecture the new members on their lack of parliamentary manners. He took issue with her right away over her defence of a private enterprise economy, announcing himself as a member from a city whose electorate had just passed judgement against such a system, perhaps a pardonable overstatement since Labour's vote in Glasgow had been just over 41 per cent of the total cast. Tackling the theme of post-war unemployment, he challenged the view that any solution to it lay in contrived efforts to revive trade with Central Europe by credit grants to potential exporters there. It was Britain's own workless who had the first claim to credit, he declared, in order to bring them back into the market as consumers. Under-consumption resulting from unemployment and a further lowering of consumer demand would be at the centre of many more speeches by Wheatley in Parliament and articles in the press.

Turning to his own local knowledge, he told the House of Glasgow's crying need for rehousing and new building which could not be undertaken by the cartels and trusts who controlled the supply and the price of building materials. As demand grew for such materials in response to post-war housing plans, so the price was pushed up further until building virtually stopped. 'Private enterprise', he finished by saying, was 'a hopeless failure with defunct machinery which can no longer operate; the longer you defend it, the more oppression and the more misery, poverty, degradation and death you will impose upon the British people.'[2]

Housing was the subject on which Wheatley spoke most often in these first months in Parliament, arming himself each time with information drawn from his own passionate involvement in Labour's campaigns over the past decade against Glasgow's landlords and building companies. Housing costs there, he pointed out, had risen fivefold since before the war, out of all proportion to labour costs, while the council faced huge post-war increases in the interest it paid on such houses as it could build. Local authorities, in Glasgow and elsewhere, must be given statutory powers to take over building land at no more than its existing valuation, while as to materials, the same principles should apply as to shell production during the war. Only by such means, he insisted, could the enormity of housing problems like those of Glasgow be tackled. He quoted the city's 1919 returns to the government on its immediate housing needs. These had listed 57,000 new houses needed, and 5,000 each year needing renewal and repair. Yet since then, just 1,500 houses had been built in Glasgow, with another 2,500 under construction. The obstacles were not, in Wheatley's view, far to seek. In his own Shettleston constituency he cited the substantial land owned for forty years by Lord Newlands, most of it registered at only token value on the city's valuation rolls. When the council's housing committee announced that it wanted to buy the land for house-building, Lord Newlands promptly clapped on to each acre a charge of £714, even though the site was earmarked for housing demobilised soldiers.

Before Wheatley's entry to Parliament, Scottish judges had, of course, found in favour of tenants evicted for rent arrears where no statutory notice to quit had accompanied actual rent increases. These judgements, endorsed on appeal and, indeed, by the House of Lords, left a substantial group of tenants in a position to retrieve additional rental payments wrongfully exacted from them. The government's 1923 legislation sought to amend existing law in order that property owners could be extricated from payment of this debt. Wheatley argued that this amounted simply to the party in power over-riding the authority of the courts in order to restore to landlords the weapon of eviction with all the havoc it could create in working-class communities.

Neville Chamberlain, the health minister, believed the Addison subsidies to be inflationary and wanted to shift more of the initiative for house-building to private enterprise. A limited subsidy went with Chamberlain's scheme to private and public builders alike over a twenty-year period, though on terms preferential to the private developers. Types of houses offered under the scheme, and the living space within them, were calculated very much on the basis of spending power. The smallest houses, 'non-parlour' houses in departmental jargon, were for those who could not afford anything, and the scheme was a buyers' one which gave little benefit to industrial workers.

Wheatley was asked by the Labour front bench to move the formal opposition amendment to the Chamberlain Bill at its second reading. His critique of what he saw as the Bill's shortcomings was a detailed one. It failed, he argued, to confront essential problems like the price of building land and materials, let alone the heavy burden of interest payable on virtually every house built. To set them against the Bill's limited provisions, he quoted once more Glasgow's statistics of housing need. What effect, he went on to ask the House, would the bill have on those areas of Lanarkshire and Fife where almost 70 per cent of all the housing stock comprised one- and two-room dwellings? He spoke of a recent incest case tried at the High Court in Edinburgh in order to remind members what some of the results of gross family overcrowding could be. In an emotional passage, he referred to his own upbringing:

> If I attempted it, I could shock even Hon. Members on the other
> side of the House by a narrative of what life means under those
> conditions. But I would say to Hon. Members that not merely do
> you not understand the housing problem, but you do not under-
> stand the intense and imperishable hatred of your social order that
> is bred in the breasts of the victims of these housing conditions.[3]

On the economics of the bills proposals, he deployed more
ammunition culled from his experience in Glasgow where soar-
ing interest rates and overpriced materials were an impediment
to the employment of building workers on desperately needed
new housing. Intervention to break the power of the price-
rings in the private building industry had now become a political imperative in its own right: 'You will be driven', he told
Chamberlain, 'to produce homes for heroes in exactly the same
way as you were driven to produce shells for heroes.'[4]

Chamberlain's bill, moreover, could only produce local
authority houses at rents beyond the reach of most wage-earners, since it did not tackle the real problem of housing costs.
Remembering his own childhood in a Lanarkshire pit row,
Wheatley questioned the Ministry of Health's criteria where
living space was concerned. Where houses were to be built
with parlours, Chamberlain told Members, an adequate parlour
for local authority schemes would be 10 ft 6 in x 9 ft 3 in. 'I
wonder', Wheatley remarked in his speech, 'what were the
dimensions of the table on which the Rt. Hon. Gentleman was
writing his figures.'[5]

> Why do you propose these boxes for our people? [he went on]
> Are they inferior people to you. Are they less useful to the com-
> munity than you? All these proposals emanate from men who
> believe in their souls that Britain is a spent force and that all you
> require is some temporary measure such as this in order to house
> your old and faithful servants until by your legislation you can

shift them to the Antipodes. Fortunately, however, for Britain and, I think fortunately for the human race, control of this country and control of this empire is rapidly passing out of the hands of the people who bring a measure like this before the Members of this House][6]

The Labour opposition could not block the bill or even secure any substantial amendments to it. Chamberlain's skill in piloting the bill through all its stages smoothed the way for him to the Treasury and, ultimately, to 10 Downing Street but the tenacity of Wheatley's performance earned him ministerial responsibility for housing sooner than he could ever have imagined.

While scoring debating points effectively off government ministers, Wheatley also took into the Chamber a capacity for vituperative attack upon opponents. In February 1923, in a debate on unemployment in which he drew attention to Britain's still huge overseas investment, he drew angry protests from the government benches when he categorised their occupants as 'knaves and fools. . . the greatest enemies of the human race'.[7] This outburst seems to have prompted no reaction from the Speaker, unlike the famous scene in which Wheatley and other Clydeside MPs were to be involved a few months later.

In that same debate he was enraged even more by the token attendance on the government side of the House. Sir William Joynson-Hicks had just cast some aspersions upon those organising agitation amongst the unemployed and Wheatley's response was to point to the empty benches around the speaker and to add 'I have no doubt an investigation of the building would reveal a larger number of enthusiastic Conservative members interested in the consumption of champagne in another part of the building than those who are now studying the condition of the people outside'.[8] This brought angry points of order, but again no disciplinary action. The clear intention of the Conservative government to dismantle much of the wartime apparatus of rent restriction served, however, to enrage him to the point where he cast aside such reverence for the House which, as a new Member, he may have had. His denunciation of the bill at its third reading was a blistering performance: 'When I listened today to the beautiful prayer with which our proceedings commenced, and I thought of the work that lay before us this afternoon, I thought that that prayer might just as appropriately have been used at the beginning of a business meeting in a coiner's den or a burglar's cave.'[9]

The greatest drama in the House in which Wheatley was involved was one in which he played a supporting role to Maxton. The House was in Committee of Supply on 27 June, debating estimates submitted by the Scottish Health Department. These revealed some conspicuous reductions in conformity with government policy, and it fell to Walter Elliot to put the case for them. The debate was uneventful until Maxton rose to speak. He had recently seen his young wife die after nursing their child through a serious illness, and the thought of it was still with him as he spoke of matters like Scotland's much greater tuberculosis rate than that of England. At this point in his speech he quoted a sentence from the estimates on the government's commitment to economy, at which Sir Frederick Banbury, Member for the City of London, interjected a loud 'Hear, hear!'. Some present thought it was Banbury's tone which provoked Maxton to react as he did. John Paton claimed later that the whole episode was well rehearsed, both Maxton's part and that of Wheatley. In any event, Maxton altered the whole tempo of his speech, turning at once to his own recent bereavement, and went on to declare, 'I am not interested in the statistics of this – I am interested only in the tens of thousands of fathers and mothers tonight watching over the cots of little babies, wondering whether they are going to live or die.'[10]

What followed has often been described since. Turning directly to Banbury, in a chamber which had fallen silent in response to his visible emotion, Maxton went on to describe as murderers any who justified on grounds of economy withdrawal or reduction of milk schemes for infants and their mothers which, he maintained, would be a direct consequence of the estimates. The word was not used directly against Elliot but against Banbury, who had risen on a point of order only for Maxton to hurl the accusation directly at him. The Deputy Speaker's first reaction was to make clear to Maxton that he had the chance to withdraw what he had said, something he was clearly not going to do. MacDonald sought a way out of the confrontation by suggesting that any personal charge of murder could, indeed, be withdrawn, without the gravity of Maxton's attack upon the health estimates being in any way diluted. Maxton's reply was to repeat the identical accusation, and it was at this point that the Member for Shettleston intervened.

Disclaiming legal expertise, Wheatley gave the House his own personal understanding of what the word 'murder' meant: 'As I understand the law, if a person does an act calculated to kill anyone, even though he did not intend to murder, that person is regarded as a murderer, and in that sense I believe that the Rt. Hon. Member for the City of London is a murderer, and I repeat it. Bring back the lives of our Scottish infants and I will withdraw.'[11] This was the Deputy Speaker's cue for calling upon both Members to withdraw, which they refused to do. Both were then suspended, as were Campbell Stephen and George Buchannan, who both repeated the word 'murderer' loudly enough to lay themselves open to suspension as well.

The Times described MacDonald sitting impotently in his

place 'white with anger at the folly of his own followers',[12] and opinion was divided on the Labour benches over the scene itself and what the leadership's response ought to be. Confrontations of this kind were not the style of Willie Graham, the douce Labour Member who had captured Central Edinburgh in 1918. 'The Glasgow men have again been a little obstreperous', he confided in writing to his brother, 'but MacDonald intends, I think, to deal firmly with them this time, although there was a considerable amount of provocation in Maxton's case. The others were merely advertisement men.'[13]

Graham was wrong in anticipating punishment for the offenders, and the Parliamentary Party went no further than issuing a rebuke and leaving it at that. Wheatley was quickly in print to justify Maxton's defiance of the House and his support for him, and indeed to claim it as a positive factor in a notable Labour by-election victory at Morpeth in Northumberland. He quoted a North of England Labour Member who predicted defeat because of the scene of a day or two before: 'The people won't tolerate such conduct and will refuse to send men of the aggressive Scottish type to Westminster.' Labour voters were ready, he argued, for their representatives in Parliament to make their presence felt even if protocol was offended:[14]

> What are called 'scenes' in Parliament shock only those who are out of touch with the realities of working-class life. . . Morpeth demonstrates that English electors want more Scotch in their politics. The workers owe nothing to a capitalist Parliament and wish to pay it exactly what they owe.
>
> It is true, I believe, that the more aggressive parliamentary policy for which many Labour Members crave might prevent a number of timid Liberals joining us. I, for one, don't want Liberals to come into the Labour Party unless they are ready to leave their Liberalism outside. I have no patience with the sham respectability

that is more shocked by an outburst by David Kirkwood than by the starvation of a child.[15]

Wheatley got a hero's welcome on his return to Glasgow and packed meetings both in his constituency and the City Hall endorsed the accusations which had led to his and the other suspensions. Referring to Scotland's level of child mortality and the relationship to it of the recent scene in the Commons, he told the City Hall audience, 'They were protesting against the slaughter of the children of the poor whose lives were estimated by their commercial value to the rich.'[16]

Wheatley was not an orator of the same calibre as Maxton but, as this speech showed, he could communicate passion and generous indignation to an audience when he wanted to. He could also make people laugh. He parodied government spokesmen who had recently attempted to explain Scotland's high child mortality figures in terms of climatic differences from England. The answer to this was the obvious one of breaking down mortality figures between selected localities and, on this basis he could observe to the City Hall audience how much superior the Kelvingrove climate must be to that of Govan.

The suspensions were lifted in due course, though not before Wheatley heard confidentially that this was the intention of the Commons. Fenner Brockway was in close touch with him at this time and later recalled how Wheatley was of the opinion that they should still exploit the situation by demanding reinstatement. With this end in view, he, Maxton and the others arrived in Palace Yard to be stopped by police, reporters and photographers. 'The confrontation was interrupted', Brockway later recalled, 'by MPs arriving from the chamber to report that the House had just agreed to withdraw the exclusion order. Rather unfairly the press and, public thought that the three rebels had forced the concession – Wheatley was a master of public relations.'[17]

Much press comment on this episode was adamant on Wheatley's controlling influence behind it: 'The strategy of the Scots is in the hands of Mr Wheatley',[18] a *Daily Dispatch* commentator assured his readers. H. N. Brailsford, editing the *New Leader*, took a similar view and, while wholly sympathetic on the issue of the Scottish Health Department's estimates, gave only guarded support to the tactics of confrontation in Parliament: 'Now it may be true that a scene, followed by agitation wins support among masses whom we reach slowly, if at all, in other ways. But there are the gravest dangers to this course; such scenes would pall if they became frequent. To keep up the stimulus you must increase the dose.'[19]

II

The 1922–23 Parliament had to invest much of its time dealing with the aftermath of the Irish settlement imposed in 1921 by the Lloyd George government. Everything in Wheatley's background made him suspicious of the new Unionist state created in the north, and within a few weeks of taking his seat he was asking leading questions about estimates under which certain Northern Irish local authorities would be relieved by the British Treasury of extra policing costs which they had incurred during the troubles since partition. He dared to question the generous pensions awarded to former senior officers of the Royal Irish Constabulary, comparing these with what was on offer to unemployed and pensioned-off workers. Arrests of Irish republican sympathisers in Britain continued well after the completion of the treaty negotiations and the ending of the Civil War in the new Free State. Many of these were deported either to the Free State or Northern Ireland, and in May 1923 special legislation was presented to Parliament to indemnify all those involved in making such arrests and deportations, not to mention those who had acted under the Restoration of Order in Ireland Act of 1920. Wheatley was active in the opposition to this legislation, stressing the financial loss to Irish people who had been victimised since 1920 by arrest, detention and deportation from Britain. At the very least, he argued, they should be able to seek compensation through civil actions against the authorities, but a Labour amendment to this made no headway.

In this period of his parliamentary apprenticeship Wheatley's preoccupations were not exclusively domestic. The ILP had worked hard to ensure its own separate representation at the new Socialist International which much of Europe's non- communist left had come together to create since the Soviet state's emergence. Wheatley was chosen as one of the party's nine delegates to attend the new International's inaugural conference at Hamburg. Before the conference took place, however, France sent troops into the Ruhr to enforce its claims to German reparation payments under the Versailles treaty. The Germans answered with strikes and passive resistance, the value of the mark tumbled once again and Britain, in A. J. P. Taylor's words, 'protested and acquiesced',[20] letting French units move to the Ruhr through an area of the Rhineland occupied by British troops. MacDonald led Labour's attempts to influence a conciliatory outcome to this crisis, urging the Bonar Law government to distance itself from France's unilateral action.

Wheatley got the chance to view this crisis at close quarters. After attending as a delegate at the Hamburg Conference, he visited the Ruhr along with Maxton, David Kirkwood and Campbell Stephen. In a report which they drew up they stressed that living conditions for the working population in many areas of Glasgow were worse than what they had seen in Germany, and Kirkwood certainly had reached the point where he felt the Labour leadership's international preoccupations were an inheritance from liberalism which was in danger of distracting it from its real tasks at home.

Wheatley was of the opinion that no British interest would be served by putting pressure on the French to withdraw and he declared himself indifferent as to whether French or German capital controlled the Ruhr. British capitalism, he maintained, preferred German control, for fear of a united Ruhr–Alsace bloc dominating the coal and steel market. The delegation's report went on to urge that the status of the Ruhr be internationalised and its profits used to clear Germany's reparation liabilities. The report was a rushed job and was criticised for lack of clarity, for example on whether the whole territory was to be given international status or just its mines and steel mills. The composition of any trust to administer on an interim basis either all the Ruhr or just its industrial plant had not been considered either. The *New Leader* was dismissive of the whole exercise: 'Nothing in this vague, hasty document tempts us to explore its suggestions further, but one laughable feature haunts the fancy. We should like to hear Mr David Kirkwood commenting in his best Bannockburn manner on a proposal to internationalize the Scottish coalfields.'[21]

Wheatley was not deterred by these attacks and was quick to intervene when the Commons debated the Ruhr crisis. Britain, he argued, occupied no pinnacle of moral superiority from which to lecture France, having been prompt enough itself to seize other German assets, like their fleet and their African colonies in 1918. He reiterated his case for international control as a way of removing any danger to British industry's competitive position, and challenged the need for Britain to get involved at all on behalf of a Ruhr population better housed and clothed than most of his own constituents in Shettleston.

This first foray into European affairs put him at odds with most Labour thinking on the peace terms. The Glasgow Trades Council condemned the concept of non-interventionism: 'The principles of Socialism would be denied and therefore fail at home, were we to leave our fellow workers in other lands to the tender mercies of the Versailles peace',[22] and the Glasgow ILP Federation submitted a motion to the party's 1923 conference condemning French action in the Ruhr in unequivocal terms. When the conference debated European policy, Wheatley, supported by Maxton, reiterated his views on the Ruhr. He was replying to a speech by H. N. Brailsford, eloquent in its defence of Labour's policy of ending the victimisation of the new German Republic under the terms of a punitive peace treaty. Wheatley moved the debate onto broader ground, rejecting the view that chaos in the Ruhr would adversely affect British trade outlets and so increase unemployment: 'He did not agree that the ruin of Europe was responsible for the unemployment and misery of Great Britain.'[23] Taken as a whole, the speech provided more than a little evidence of the growing influence upon Wheatley of under-consumptionist economic theory and the belief that rational management of credit and investment offered the best hope of reviving domestic demand in Britain.

Clifford Allen, ILP Treasurer, followed Wheatley and returned to the attack on his proposals for internationalising the Ruhr. Once more, Scottishness was a weapon with which Wheatley and his colleagues were belaboured: 'He [Allen] had heard something about Home Rule for Scotland. When they began to talk about internationalizing other parts of the earth, he thought charity began at home.'[24] Wheatley found himself on the losing side of this debate because the peace settlement was still an emotional subject for the ILP, and Allen was a formidable opponent in debate, personifying as he did so much of the strength of Labour's internationalism. His analysis of the world economy's relationship to British problems carried more weight with delegates than Wheatley's arguments, which could be attacked for having within them an element of what could be represented as a selfish socialism concerned to tackle capitalist problems within national state frontiers.

Before the March 1923 ILP Conference, Wheatley had published an eight-page pamphlet setting out his views on the broader issue of Britain's post-war economic decline and the growing unemployment which was its most obvious symptom. Wheatley's intention, however, was to show that unemployment was not merely a symptom but a significant factor which accelerated decline by bringing about a progressive lowering of consumer demand. *Starving in the Midst of Plenty* was the title he gave this pamphlet, for his central concern in it was to show that the resources for economic recovery lay within Britain itself, and in an abundance that made nonsense of the thesis that wages must be held down and public expenditure cut. In it he wrote:

> If Britain is to regain its proud position as workshop of the world, British workers must accept the Coolie standard of wages. Having reduced British wages, Britain again becomes the world's workshop and closes the Indian workshops. After a time the Coolie is forced to accept less rice in order that he may regain a place in the sun. On lower wages the Indian factories re-open and Lord Weir's factories go on short time. The next step is, of course, a further reduction in British wages until the last straw is reached. Then, when the futility of this policy is apparent to the most foolish, the workers are told they must leave their native land.[25]

Emigration schemes, funded and publicised in a variety of ways by government, became a particular target for Wheatley. In *Starving in the Midst of Plenty* he attacked them with more than a touch of xenophobia: 'Frequently, as was remarked by one of my colleagues in the House of Commons, emigration is insolently advocated by men who speak English with difficulty.'[26] In essence, his remedy was influenced very clearly by his assimilation of the under-consumptionist economic theory which J. A. Hobson had been developing since his *Imperialism* first came out in 1902. State action must revive economic growth and redistributive taxation must increase the workers' spending power. Huge inequalities like those dividing Glasgow's East End from its West End were not only immoral, they were an irrational impediment to economic recovery: 'Those who need the goods haven't the purchasing power and those who have the purchasing power don't need the goods. So the goods remain unbought and the needy look on and starve.'[27]

Taking shape here was the idea of a British road, if not to socialism, then to the revival of the British economy by the restructuring of national income through progressive taxation which would create new working-class spending power more readily than any export drive. Exception has been taken by some writers to what they see as Wheatley's use of racial stereotypes in this leaflet as well as what seems to them his view that Labour's first duty was to workers in Britain rather than to those of other races. In fact, it is debateable whether the word 'coolie' was always, or necessarily, used in a racist sense in this period, and Wheatley was arguing that if the battle for exports was accepted as the cure to Britain's post-war economic problems, then workers of all races would be the losers in a descending spiral of competitive wage cuts.

He could pursue the argument now through other outlets because he had begun to write for the *New Leader* under an editor of eclectic talents, H. N. Brailsford. Returning to his theme of the importance of revived domestic demand, he declared in one of his articles that our difficulties do not arise in the main from a collapse of our foreign trade but are the direct consequence of the breakdown of our trade with the British working class. . . the pressing duty of the British Labour Party is to reconstruct our social system so that the entire population may be put in a position to purchase goods as rapidly as they can be produced. By concentrating on this we would do much more to bring peace and prosperity to Europe than we can possibly do by attempting to reconcile the continuous conflicts of international capitalism.[28]

For Wheatley, his first session in Parliament could not have been fuller. Over and above his active attendance at the House, he was, with Dollan, elected to the ILP's National Administrative Council, the body which existed to implement party policy as formulated at annual or special conferences of delegates. He had already attended one of the ILP's celebrated Summer Schools in 1922 before his election to Parliament, and took part in another the next year. These were held at Easton Lodge, the country home of the maverick Countess of Warwick, and were important in the ILP's development as an intellectual force. For Wheatley, they were a way of widening his intellectual circle through the debates and discussions which were usually attended by celebrity guest speakers like Brailsford, H. G. Wells, Shaw and John Maynard Keynes. Their influence upon Wheatley began to be apparent in his concern to become an authority on more than just Glasgow's health and housing problems.

III

At the ILP's Conference it was Wheatley who moved a resolution not initially on the conference agenda. His resolution read as follows: 'That this conference recommends that Labour MPs shall not accept hospitality from political opponents at public dinners and society functions except where it may be necessary for the Leader of the Party to meet the King on state occasion.'[29] This was carried after a debate by ninety-three votes to ninety but not before Wheatley agreed to delete from his motion the section referring to the King (i.e. the words from 'functions' to the end). Some delegates had argued that the original wording implied that the King was a political opponent of Labour. The conference chairman, R. C. Wallhead, accepted this as a point of order, adding that the King is apart from politics and cannot be regarded as an opponent'. This has been interpreted by some as proof of an inflexible attitude by Wheatley and the Clydeside MPs to social contacts with those who did not share their views. Many of them saw Parliament as 'territory occupied by the class enemy, as a capitalist institution'[30] behind the rituals and the social life that emanated from it. 'John, we'll soon change all this',[31] David Kirkwood had said audibly to Wheatley as they stood at the bar of the House of Lords for the royal speech to open the 1923 session. Wheatley's first session in Parliament showed that he was undeceived by many of its pretensions and stuffier traditions, but was prepared to use it as a forum within which to attack Labour's opponents with increasing effect and voice his own developing political ideas.

In London, too, he could afford, unlike the rest of the Clydeside group, to maintain a life-style which, while by no means lavish, enabled him to mix socially during the week with journalists like Hobson and Brailsford, and the radical Liberal MP Charles Masterman. Masterman was a frequent contributor of articles to the *Nation* and Wheatley came to form a close working relationship with him during the short lifetime of the first Labour government. Unlike Maxton, Campbell Stephen and George Buchanan, who shared flats or digs, Wheatley, once in Parliament, could afford to stay in private hotels, usually the 'Cosmo' in Southampton Row, whose writing paper he quite often used for such of his correspondence as survives. From there he would usually travel by bus to Westminster, often lunching nearby and taking an evening meal in his hotel or in local restaurants. Often these meals were taken with the other Glasgow MPs, virtually always without alcohol. John McGovern, in his time chairman of Shettleston Constituency Labour Party and later an MP, did recall one weakness of Wheatley that remained with him from his days as a miner, that of placing the occasional bet. McGovern wrote of one meal where, forgetting it was Friday, Wheatley had ordered a steak after news of a win. Wheatley was reminded by George Buchannan of what day it was but decided the church would give him a dispensation in the circumstances.

Wheatley's Glasgow commitments remained, of course, both in his Shettleston constituency, where throughout the session he was a regular speaker at Saturday and Sunday meetings, and in his firm Hoxton and Walsh, which continued to expand its operations and its turnover. In 1916 the Glasgow Trades Council had given it the contract for printing all its publicity material, and many more contracts from church bodies and local business came in. This expansion, however, had not been accomplished without tension.

In early 1917, it appears that M'Gettigan, his pre-war friend and business partner, wanted to dissolve the company and retire from it, while Wheatley wanted to increase the share capital of what was becoming a successful business. The disagreement between them over the firm's future involved legal action, with a court carrying out the formal procedure of liquidation in 1918 as a result of deadlock between the two partners. Wheatley, however, was able to purchase the goodwill of the company for £100 from the liquidator and re-form Hoxton and Walsh as his own company with a nominal share capital of £5,000. Under Wheatley's sole control the business continued to expand and in 1921 its turnover was more than £71,000. With a view to getting Hoxton and Walsh more fully capitalised, Wheatley contacted Rosslyn Mitchell, the solicitor and active ILP member. Mitchell was successful in securing the help of another Irish immigrant's son, Thomas White, a successful solicitor closely associated with the Glasgow Celtic Football Club. His financial backing was conditional upon Wheatley's willingness to stay with Hoxton and Walsh for a minimum of ten years. White's financial support was important in getting many of his Catholic publican clients to invest in the firm.

One of these investors was James McVey, a wholesale wine merchant and traveller for a brewing firm who had financial interests in several public houses in the East End of Glasgow. When, in 1920, Hoxton and Walsh's capital was increased to £25,000, McVey purchased 2,750 one-pound shares. His involvement with the firm was later to become a blunt-edged weapon in the hands of Wheatley's political opponents.

In 1923 Wheatley felt able to draw upon his capital to launch a paper which was to become an important outlet for his views on national questions, and in which his major speeches in Parliament and the country were often printed. This was the *Glasgow Eastern Standard*, a paper which survived until 1960 and which was, in its time, a vigorous and comprehensive community weekly as well as being a vehicle for Wheatley's ideas. Two other local papers also published by Hoxton and Walsh were the *Glasgow Southside Standard* and the *Glasgow Eastern Star*, and ultimately the company had quite extensive publishing interests and subsidiaries which it controlled in Scotland, some English cities and Ireland. Among these were the Ecclesiastical Press and the Edgar Printing and Publishing Company.

By the time he became an MP, Wheatley was a comparatively wealthy man, able to pay for a university education for his son and daughter, and soon to buy a substantial house overlooking the Sandyhills golf-course in Shettleston. The paradox of his militant politics and secure finances and prosperous bourgeois appearance was lost neither on him nor his opponents. His spectacles, good suits and his tendency to corpulence made him an easy target for cartoonists. Yet this was a man who never forgot the poverty he had escaped nor forgave a social system which continued to inflict such deprivation as it did on the working class in Scotland and Britain as a whole. His memories from Baillieston and the pits left him with a generous anger at injustice that would remain his central point of reference for all that he sought to achieve in Parliament.

IV

A premature end came to the Parliament elected in December 1922 by Baldwin's decision that he would not tackle unemployment without a wide measure of trade protection. He made this conversion public on 25 October 1923, along with his intention to honour Bonar Law's pledge, made in the previous general election, that no change in fiscal policy would be made without another appeal to the electorate. However, Baldwin had already told Tom Jones of his determination to outflank Lloyd George before the latter went protectionist himself. Tariffs might also restore relationships with former Conservative Coalitionists like Austen Chamberlain and Lord Birkenhead (F. E. Smith) as well as securing the Conservative majority won the previous year. Baldwin's political judgement had, in fact, deserted him, for polling on 6 December opened the way to office for Britain's first Labour government.

Labour in Scotland had to fight its second general election in barely a year on a tight budget, but managed to put up candidates in forty-nine of the seventy-one seats. Opposed only by a Liberal in Shettleston, Wheatley in his speeches poured scorn on the sham alternatives of protectionism and Free Trade. The economy's real problem, he argued, was the under-consumption of goods and services which poverty itself created, and the resulting vicious circle would remain unbreakable until there were state initiatives in demand management, redistributive taxation and measures to fund economic growth. Against this, Free Trade was the ethos of capitalism undefiled, while protectionism was the hypocrisy of those who objected to cheap goods produced by exploited labour only when this happened overseas. The danger for Labour, he claimed, was that much of its thinking on the economy was still unformed and was a prey to the influence of the two capitalist parties. 'Labour is only a Socialist party in the making', he wrote in *Forward* on the eve of the campaign. 'Many of its ingredients are still adulterated with Liberalism.'[32] The real counter-weight to forces that would impede Labour's socialist development was, he believed, the ILP: 'The ILP is called to save the Labour movement again as it did in the war days. We are not Free Traders, we are not Protectionists. We are not neutral. We are Socialists with a Socialist policy. We won't be led into following either Liberalism or Toryism.'[33]

Wheatley held his Shettleston seat with a majority of 4,153, a reduction from the year before. He polled 12,624 votes, against his opponent's 8,471 and was one of 191 Labour members to be returned, along with 258 Conservatives and 159 Liberals. This result made it clear that the Conservatives unaided could not for long remain in office once Parliament assembled in the New Year. Nontheless, there was enough talk of a Liberal–Tory coalition in order to keep Labour out of power to draw Wheatley's scorn, especially for the Liberals.

Liberalism, he declared, had now acted out its historical role: 'Dressed in its old garments it struts the stage as a lover of liberty; but we have reached the point where Liberalism and Toryism, like the Colonel's Lady and Judy O'Grady, are sisters under the skin.'[34]

In the same article, Wheatley dismissed the notion of Labour settling for office on the basis of sharing it with the Liberals: 'Such a coalition or compromise is impossible. Were it possible, and adopted, it would break the hearts of those gallant men and women whose sacrifices and enthusiasm have carried our movement to the gates of the promised land.'[35] The promised land in 1924 and subsequently may have eluded Labour, but Wheatley was clear in his own mind that MacDonald should stake out Labour's claim to office if it could bring down Baldwin and command a majority in the Commons.

He was adamant, too, that Labour must not show itself infirm of purpose or fearful of the forces that would be arrayed against it:

> It would be political madness to leave the impression in the public mind that the Labour movement is not a menace to vested interests. These interests are keeping our people in the depths of poverty and are now actually threatening to throttle our national existence. We must destroy them rapidly in self-preservation. The people of Glasgow will support us in this task and so will every other section of the populace, if we nail our colours to the mast and leave timidity to the rear.[36]

This uncompromising rhetoric no doubt strengthened the resolve of many of Wheatley's colleagues in the Commons when, on 21 January, they went into the lobbies with the Liberals to bring Baldwin's government down. For Wheatley himself the challenge of matching rhetoric to the hard realities of office in a minority Labour government was now just hours away.

7 The 1924 Labour government

Wheatley suffered some uncertainty from MacDonald's formation of his government, for the leader was preoccupied with what he felt was Labour's lack of experience. Writing to Arthur Henderson in December 1923 he confided that, 'I have to admit that we are terribly short of men. There is no use our blinking the fact. We shall have to put into some of the offices men who are not only untried but whose capacity to face the permanent officials is very doubtful,'[1] His first choice for Health Minister was Charles Trevelyan, the former Liberal, and Wheatley was offered only the position of Parliamentary Under-Secretary at the Ministry.

Wheatley's prompt refusal of this junior position, clearly backed by the Clyde group of MPs, seems to have forced MacDonald's hand, and the same day, 22 January, he accepted the offer to become Health Minister. MacDonald's diary reveals his doubts about the matter: 'Wheatley finally fixed. Necessary to bring the Clyde in. Will he play straight?'[2] Wheatley, himself, did not feel strong enough to make an issue of Maxton's exclusion from the cabinet. All Maxton was offered was the position of Parliamentary Under-Secretary in Wheatley's Ministry. MacDonald, it has been suggested, was receptive to 'the fear of Anglo-Saxons of too many Scots in the Cabinet'.[3]

MacDonald must have felt confirmation of his doubts when Wheatley announced that he would not wear court dress for the swearing-in of the new government. He was supported in this by Tom Shaw, a Lancashire textile trade unionist and Minister of Labour designate, though he was on the party's right. MacDonald already felt under pressure due to the King's unease at a rendering of the 'Red Flag' at a recent Labour election celebration in the Albert Hall, but was unable to make Wheatley change his mind. The outcome mattered little, for the new Health Minister knelt with his colleagues to kiss the monarch's hand in the approved manner. George V, himself, made a subsequent note of his first individual audience with Wheatley: 'Received Mr Wheatley, the Minister of Health. He is an extreme Socialist and comes from Glasgow. I had a very interesting conversation with him.'[4]

Wheatley was contemptuous, however, of attempts to initiate the new ministers into some of the mysteries and refinements of the London social scene. Beatrice Webb was a prime mover in these exercises, which had been going on intermittently since 1922, to rub the real or imagined rough edges off Labour MPs. To those who thought like her, the task took on an added urgency with Labour in office. Operating through what was called the Half-Circle Club, these well-wishers of Labour set out to teach some ministers, and also their wives, how to balance a teacup and saucer in polite company and the correct angle at which to crook the little finger.

Wheatley remained impervious to this patronising nonsense. He liked to circulate the story of how a countess had expressed in a letter to his wife her great disappointment at not having met her at some social function involving ministers in the new government. The letter went on to inform his wife that the countess would be at home the following Tuesday. Mrs Wheatley sent a reply saying that she would also be at home that day, in the family house in Shettleston. John Scanlon suggested that she might have added for the benefit of the countess that Tuesday was a washing day in Glasgow.

Wheatley's freedom of action in the cabinet remained in doubt, given that MacDonald used the cabinet committee system as a counter-weight to the Clydeside socialism that the new Minister of Health might be likely to apply through his department. Webb, then Snowden, were appointed by the Prime Minister as chairmen of the Housing and Unemployment Committee, while Haldane, the Lord Chancellor and a recent convert from liberalism, was given the chair of the Home Affairs Committee.

The Ministry of Health had come into existence very much as a product of the determination of the Liberal, Christopher Addison. As Minister of Reconstruction in the Coalition, he had fought tenaciously in the final months of the war to secure a commitment from Lloyd George to a central department of state with co-ordinating powers over health and housing policy. Addison was appointed Britain's first Health Minister in June 1919 and at once had an attritional fight on his hands. Bodies with Poor Law, health and housing functions, notably the Local Government and Education Board, resented the new ministry. Financial assistance for local council slum clearance and house-building was central to Addison's conception of his ministry's role and, in June 1921, feeling isolated and betrayed by Lloyd George, he resigned, though not before the foundations for a post-war subsidised housing strategy had been laid. In fact, the number of houses built between the summers of 1920 and 1921 was the largest in any single year between the world wars, apart from 1928, when the benefits of Wheatley's own legislation were emerging. Wheatley admired Addison's resistance to Treasury cost-cutting and his commitment to a central housing role for local authorities. On taking office himself in 1924, Wheatley wrote to Addison, 'You had no greater admirer than I during your period at the Ministry of Health.'[5]

Some observers were confident that Wheatley would make

an impact, even allowing for the constraints upon a minority government. In a profile of him written in 1924, Mary Agnes Hamilton, after recalling his career in Glasgow Labour politics, wrote:

> In appearance rather like the traditional Mr Pickwick, his is the iron hand in the velvet glove. His power over his Scottish colleagues is remarkable. To the Ministry of Health he brings the authority of an expert: he finds there an opportunity of immediate constructive work such as is open to none of his Cabinet colleagues.[6]

John Scanlon, a Glasgow socialist journalist and former shipyard worker, who for a time worked closely with Wheatley as a personal secretary, received a summons from him on his first day in office. 'I remember', Scanlon wrote later, 'the first day he was appointed Minister of Health. He phoned me saying he would like a talk. We met at his little room in Southampton Row and almost the first thing he said was: "Get your brainbox working. Clear from your mind any ideas that you will get any Socialism. What can we do that will be worthwhile for the workers of Britain?"' Scanlon's answer was that the first requirement for a Labour government was to draw up an inventory of Britain's wealth, who created it and how it was distributed:

> In that little hotel we jotted down all the lines of the possible enquiry. . . A long sheet of paper was filled in asking for details of all the sources of Britain's wealth. Who got it ? How was it shared; and when that was known, was it essential that some must be hungry and some get indigestion from overeating?[7]

The exercise was quite in keeping with Wheatley's own concern never to let day-to-day political concerns crowd out the broader view. In relation, however, to the pressures of actual office in a minority administration, the document roughed out

by the new minister and John Scanlon would have little significance outside their hotel room in Southampton Row. Wheatley
decided quickly what his own priorities as a minister would
have to be, though he was never to lose his capacity to assimi-
late ideas that would enable him to look and think beyond the
details of specific proposals.

Wheatley's first controversial decision was, in fact, not long
in coming and arose from a sequence of events dating from
well before his taking office. These had centred upon the East
London Borough of Poplar, where Labour had won control of
both the Poor Law Board of Guardians and the council. Under
George Lansbury's leadership, Labour gave spending priority to
local needs and refused to draw upon Poplar's thinly stretched
resources to meet a London County Council precept which
would contribute to the funding of boroughs infinitely better
off than Poplar.

In early 1921 the Coalition Health Minister, Sir Alfred
Mond, had issued a statutory order limiting severely the scales
of unemployment relief which the Poplar Board of Guardians
could operate. It was for defiance of this order that the Poplar
Guardians chose to go to prison, but even after that they managed to make the Mond Order virtually inoperable by the
number of special benefit claims they referred upwards to the
Health Ministry. Joynson-Hicks, Mond's successor, was preparing to suspend the Poplar Board of Guardians when Parliament
was dissolved in November 1923. He was also preparing surcharges on them for the illegal unemployment rates of benefit
they had been paying along with the £4 minimum wage they
had sanctioned in their capacity as councillors for those
employed by the Borough of poplar.

Wheatley had denounced this threat in opposition and one
of his first decisions as minister was to receive a deputation
from the Poplar Board of Guardians on 5 February 1924. Their

demands were threefold: they wanted the Mond Order rescinded; they wanted remission of surcharges made upon them for allegedly paying unemployment benefit without due regard to a whole family's resources; and they wanted remission of any surcharges arising from the Poplar policy of paying a £4 minimum wage to those in the Board's employment. He had to answer that he could not act on their second and third demands, since the legal implications were still under review and in the case of the minimum wage, due to be tested before a court. On the central issue of the Mond Order, he made it clear that his mind was already made up and that he would rescind it forthwith and cancel any surcharges made under it. No sooner, moreover, had he and the deputation parted than he made his decision known to the press in an official statement.

At the cabinet meeting three days later, Wheatley was reprimanded for his action, though without being named, the minutes referring to the Prime Minister's strong appeal to his colleagues not to make announcements on controversial matters without consulting him first. This still left MacDonald with the dilemma of whether to repudiate his minister's initiative, or to let it appear that he, too, endorsed the way Poplar had defied the courts. The best way out presented itself to him as getting Wheatley's agreement to a further public statement playing down the Mond Order as in any case unworkable. Wheatley duly made this statement, stressing that his rescinding of the Order did 'not involve or imply any general alteration in Poor Law Policy'.[8]

Denunciations of Wheatley's actions came thick and fast from the opposition parties and the press, and a full-scale challenge in the Commons became unavoidable with *The Times* even speculating on the likely fall of MacDonald's government. A debate was agreed for 26 February on a Liberal motion of censure on Wheatley to which the Conservatives added a strongly worded amendment. This was easily enough defeated by Labour and Liberal members voting together and Wheatley's defence of his actions over Poplar was instrumental in getting the Liberal motion withdrawn. His speech was, in Philip Snowden's view, a 'veritable triumph'.[9] Snowden recalled Asquith saying after the debate that never in all his time in the House had he heard a minister defend himself with such skill. Beatrice Webb entered in her diary after the Poplar debate that Wheatley was 'a new star in House of Commons dialectics, logical and humorous with first-rate delivery. . . he takes his place as a frontranker in the game, a rival to Thomas for the leadership if JRM breaks down'.[10]

He made a careful tactical choice of ground. Mond's Poplar Order, he argued, had become inoperable almost from the moment of being issued. Three previous Health Ministers he quoted as having admitted this but having lacked the courage either to enforce the order or to rescind it. Surcharges pending under the order had, in effect, already been remitted, and grants-in aid from central government had continued to be paid to the Board of Guardians. 'I have not surrendered to Poplar', he declared, 'I do not intend to surrender to Poplar. I have, however, rescued my Department from a state of degradation. I have put my Department in a position in which it can and will enforce the law and will do so fearlessly.'[11]

Such a line of defence was cleverly conceived to neutralise charges of condoning illegality and took the pressure off the government. MacDonald was left to sum up the debate by offering little more than a résumé of his Health Minister's speech, reiterating that 'Poplarism' had not been sanctioned and that a Joint or Select Committee of the House would explore the issue more fully. He made little reference to Wheatley's strong defence of local democracy in his speech and his adamant rejection of the demand that he should have used his ministerial powers to suspend the Poplar Guardians.

Within a cabinet where he had to reckon on a majority against any seeming endorsement of illegality, Wheatley had to reiterate the departmental view that 'any expenditure on relief which is excessive or unlawful whether incurred by Poplar or any other Board of Guardians, will continue to be liable to disallowance and surcharge'.[12] Free of the constraints of office at the end of the year, his tone was a different one. He received a hero's welcome in Poplar when he arrived there to open a new block of flats. He admitted to 'great joy and pride in being associated with Poplarism' and went on to say that 'only as the policy of Poplar permeated the country would they march towards a different order of society'.[13]

George Lansbury remained grateful to Wheatley for what he had done, though accepting the constraints within which he had to operate:

> I ought to put on record the fact that John Wheatley, when he became Minister of Health, by a stroke of the pen wiped out surcharges amounting to thousands of pounds and repealed a ridiculous order issued against us by Sir Alfred Mond. In many ways he lightened our task as far as it was possible to do so by administrative act.[14]

The Poplar crisis had exposed a new and inexperienced Labour government to severe attack, but Wheatley had carried out a skilful exercise in damage limitation without compromising on his own support for elected local bodies. The campaign of support for the Poplar Guardians and councillors was not one Wheatley would have denounced, given his own experience of community-based direct action in Glasgow on issues like house rents. Difficulties with Poplar and other like-minded London localities would remain, he pointed out to MacDonald in a 7 March memo, for so long as the government of London and the administration of the Poor Law itself remained unchanged. He was, in fact, made chairman of a cabinet committee on Poor Law reform, but there was time for it to hold only one meeting in August before the defeat of the government.

The cabinet was also confronted with the operation of the Poor Law in the different context of strikes and the way that relief to strikers and their families should be administered, if indeed any should be paid at all. The definitive statement of English law on this was a 1900 judgement under which a High Court injunction was awarded to an employer against a South Wales Board of Guardians (Merthyr Tydfil) to restrain them from paying out relief to strikers. Boards like Poplar had breached this ruling, but the Ministry of Health could do little in such a situation except wait for the District Auditor to disallow the expenditure involved, which, of course, could lead to a surcharge upon any offending Board of Guardians.

The outbreak of a dock strike soon after Labour took office affected areas where Labour Boards of Guardians had already paid out benefit to strikers. This forced Wheatley to prepare for the cabinet a review of departmental thinking on the whole issue. This reiterated the law as it stood, which was that a strike did not 'give to the men collectively any right to relief which they would not have individually'.[15] Relief to families was possible under existing Poor Law legislation if a strike caused demonstrable hardship, but Wheatley's paper pointed out that if such relief were paid strikers could still be made liable on charges of neglect of their families under vagrancy law.

His dealings with Poplar had already made clear to him that the law itself was unevenly applied, as indeed was the 1900 Merthyr judgement: 'The difficulties of applying this judgement in practice have resulted in lack of uniformity in administration on the part of different Boards of Guardians, and have made it impossible for the Department to adopt a clear-cut policy.'[16] Beyond that, he identified the problem as one arising from the 'conflict between the contention that a strike should not be supported out of rate funds and the statutory duty of the Guardians as responsible for the relief of destitution to prevent a striker from starving. And there can, of course, be no question of allowing persons on strike to starve.'

Wheatley did not attempt to alter his ministry's policy in any fundamental way on a matter which the cabinet itself did not want to get drawn into. When his report was debated, the cabinet maintained a cautious line, agreeing that 'the Ministry of Health should issue no special circular on the subject applicable to the Dock Strike, but, if enquiries are made, they should assist local authorities to a knowledge of the law'.[17] This is not quite the same as the view put in a recent book that Wheatley was a party to an attempt to 'restrict poor-law benefit to strikers' families, which was too right-wing for the 1924 Labour Government to accept'.[18] His concern reads rather more as being to avoid administrative and legal pitfalls pending a reform of the Poor Law which a minority Labour government would not be able to undertake.

Housing was Wheatley's most urgent priority but it quickly drew him into treacherous parliamentary ground, from which he had to extricate himself with as much skill as he had shown over the Poplar episode. In Glasgow, particularly, landlords were still making ruthless use of their eviction powers under the Coalition's 1920 legislation, and a Labour back-bencher, Ben Gardner, introduced a Private Member's Bill to amend existing law in such a way as, at least, to protect the unemployed from eviction. The key clause in Gardner's bill declared that no unemployed worker in rent arrears should be evicted unless the hardship to his landlord involved in not evicting could be shown to be greater than that to the tenant if there were an eviction.

Initially, government support was not given to Gardner's bill but Wheatley was careful to discuss it with Arthur Greenwood, his Parliamentary Under-Secretary, and Sir Patrick Hastings, the Attorney-General. Wheatley's view, recorded in cabinet papers, was that the Gardner bill was quite well drafted. 'I have asked', he wrote in a cabinet memorandum of 7 March 1924, 'Greenwood to look after our interests in committee but not to make the measure a Government bill.'[19] The signs, however, soon pointed to Gardner's bill running aground in committee, a prospect that infuriated Kirkwood, in particular, who made a bitter attack on MacDonald for not backing the bill. The Prime Minister had, in fact, anticipated trouble in a letter to Wheatley's private office in the Health Ministry. Wheatley then intervened with a memorandum on evictions, arguing that the increased rate of evictions was a clear product of unemployment. At a cabinet meeting on 26 March, a government bill, based on Wheatley's document and little different from the Gardner bill, was announced; it was presented to the Commons on 2 April, far too short a time for adequate preparation or discussion, as events quickly proved.

Critics of the bill had already argued that the key clause on unemployed tenants was impractical and likely to encourage landlords to evict all tenants who seemed in danger of becoming unemployed. A vote in the Commons duly went against the government on this clause in the second reading debate. Maxton had urged that ministers treat the clause as a resignation matter. Clynes, Wheatley and a few other ministers attempted to save the bill by proposing an alternative clause which would make the maintenance of an unemployed tenant in his home a charge upon public funds. The Speaker then had to rule the new clause out of order on the grounds that it would require a Money Resolution to be voted by the whole House and, amidst growing confusion, the bill was talked out. By now the bill was past praying for, despite another attempt to relaunch it with a clause which would give local authorities a liability for meeting the rent arrears of the unemployed. The question then arose of whether grants-in-aid from central government funds would be used to assist local authorities, and ministers were back under the same line of attack when the bill was returned to the House on 7 April. Wheatley had insisted throughout that he held to the principle that responsibility for preventing the growing numbers of workless also becoming homeless was one for the whole community, not just the landlords directly involved. The whole exercise had been rushed to the point where a procedural minefield negated Wheatley's best intentions, and on 8 April the government was again defeated.

Tenant rights was an intractable problem which consumed much more of the session, but the government, its fingers burnt once, confined itself to making over such parliamentary time as it could to back-benchers, and in July a Prevention of Evictions Bill received the Royal Assent. It had little specific to say about the position of unemployed tenants and Maxton described it as 'this emaciated thing'.[20]

The whole confused episode did little for Wheatley's relations with MacDonald and exposed him to the charge that he had acted precipitately in response to pressure from the Glasgow group of MPs. Few, however, denied that Wheatley had defended his own role with a skill similar to that which he had shown in the Poplar debate a few weeks earlier. For Beatrice Webb it was 'another example of Wheatley getting the Government into a deep hole, climbing out of it himself in a brilliantly successful speech, leaving the Government still deeper down in the hole which he had made'.[21] She quoted also the view of MacDonald's secretary, who had told her husband Sidney that he

> thought the PM would not be sorry to be thrown out on this issue in order to let the Clyde men see the result of their own folly. Is he beginning to be jealous of Wheatley's damaging *réclame* in the press as the greatest Parliamentarian on the Treasury Bench? It would be unlike J.R.M. if he were not getting tired of the Clyde men and jealous of their brilliant protagonist in the cabinet.[22]

Issues like Poplar and the intractable parliamentary problems of legislation on evictions ate severely into the time Wheatley needed to prepare the housing bill which he saw as his most important task. His own knowledge of housing problems, acquired first hand in a miners' row in Baillieston and as a Glasgow councillor, had impressed upon him both the supreme urgency of getting decent houses built quickly and also the need not to court failure by neglecting to consult all parties whose co-operation would be essential if any legislation was to work. The cabinet's Housing and Unemployment Committee proved an unwieldy body, and increasingly Wheatley reported either to the full cabinet or to MacDonald individually on the preparation of his bill.

On 30 January Wheatley had his first meeting with the trade unions and major employers in the building industry in order to prepare the ground for his legislation. When he reported back to the full cabinet he ran, almost at once, into trouble with the Treasury and Philip Snowden who, as Chancellor, was already emerging as a vigilant guardian of the 'Treasury view'. Snowden warned of over-large housing targets and the drain upon funds involved in government subsidy commitments. He used his position as Chairman of the Housing and Unemployment Committee successfully to make a case for any house-building programme to be spread over fifteen years, not ten as Wheatley had first proposed. Any subsidy, Snowden insisted, was to be set at a lower figure than Wheatley had in mind and was to apply in a uniform way to each house built. Willie Gallacher put it to Wheatley that he should resign rather than accept such terms, but failed to persuade him. Thomas Jones, Secretary to the Cabinet, was of the opinion that this 'watering down of great expectations' was, in part, the work of Wheatley's departmental officials, using Arthur Greenwood, Parliamentary Under-Secretary to the Health Ministry, as their intermediary,[23] but the critical role was Snowden's rather than Greenwood's.

Losing a battle like this at the very outset prepared Wheatley all the better for the long struggle which was to follow. He had initially wanted a variable subsidy geared to local authority housing needs and population density, but stood little chance in a head-on clash with the Treasury just weeks after taking office. His first priority was to take employers and unions in the house-building industry along with his scheme, and on 6 February he and Arthur Greenwood secured their agreement to a joint committee comprising nineteen employers' representatives and fifteen representatives of the unions. Although the unions were to have the vice-chairmanship of the committee, there were Labour criticisms of its composition in the Commons, but Wheatley justified it on the grounds that Labour's purpose was not to destroy private enterprise in house-building or in the manufacture of essential building materials. Labour, he was at pains repeatedly to stress, challenged only the principle of private capital invested in the ownership of rented property: 'The Labour Party's programme on housing is not a Socialist programme at all', he told Parliament on 26 March, 'I wish it were'. He went on, 'I wish this country were ready to receive a Socialist programme and we would show you how much easier it is to solve the housing problem along those lines than trying to patch up the capitalist system of which you yourselves have made such a mess.'[24]

This was to be a recurrent theme in his many speeches on the bill's passage through Parliament. He saw the only way forward for a minority Labour government as being the development of a fruitful relationship between both sides of the building industry and the local authorities, with central government subsidising the housing programme which his scheme would make possible. He resented Neville Chamberlain's accusation that he was hostile to house ownership. Local authority house-letting, he stressed, was a transitional answer to a long-term problem created by poverty and by the failures of private building. 'I own the house I live in', he declared to Parliament, 'and I make it a rule in my public life to try to bring to others the facilities and privileges that I have myself.'[25] Wheatley's 1924 bill was not equipped to achieve that, but in the same speech he stressed how he hoped to see the day when enough houses would be built not just for letting but for sale at prices within the reach of working people who wanted to buy their homes.

On 10 April the joint committee of building unions and employers which he had set up reported back to Wheatley. It called for a government guarantee for a fifteen-year plan to build 2.5 million houses, at an annual rate rising from an initial 50,000 to 225,000. To increase recruitment to a badly depleted labour force, the committee called for the starting age limit for all apprenticeships in the industry to be raised from sixteen years to twenty, and for the period of apprenticeship to be cut from five years to three. Finally, they proposed a National House Building Committee to co-ordinate and oversee housebuilding and the placing of contracts.

Wheatley had reason to be well pleased with recommendations that matched his own thinking on the broad intent of any housing bill. As important, however, as the building industry's goodwill was that of the local authorities and he was as careful in carrying them along with every stage of his bill's preparation. In a circular letter of 12 May 1924 to all local authorities in Scotland, England and Wales, he emphasised that their autonomy under his scheme would be no less than under existing housing legislation. They would, his letter stressed, still be free to decide how many houses they would build subject to an upper limit laid down by his ministry, while the size of houses under his scheme would not be altered from the terms of the Chamberlain Act of the year before. Wheatley had been strongly critical of this part of Chamberlain's legislation in the 1923 parliament, but the local authorities, only a minority of which were Labour, made it clear that they wished to keep to the 'status quo'. Even if Wheatley could not change their minds on this, he still saw them as essential partners in the working of his scheme.

To local authorities fearful of incurring losses under his scheme, Wheatley promised that central government would cover them for up to two-thirds of such losses. In some areas, once it became clear that a major bill was in preparation, house-building came to a virtual stop as councils waited to see what their position would be in relation to actual subsidies which would be on offer if the bill was passed. This led to pressure on him to declare that the bill would be retrospective in its operation. On this, he was wisely reluctant to anticipate what Parliament's view might be, though his own preference, he made clear, was for legislation that would apply retrospectively for one month from the time of the bill's introduction to Parliament.

Wheatley's commitment to local government autonomy was wholly in character with his own earlier position in the municipal politics of Glasgow. The local authority associations accepted this in their meetings with him, but the bill was threatened when the issue of differential subsidies came up. The draft bill proposed fixed subsidies for fixed periods in urban areas and rural parishes, yet Wheatley was not the man to need reminding how much housing needs varied around the country. He was pressed hard on this by some local authority representatives, as the cabinet papers on the bill's preparation make clear, but, despite his own initial feelings, found himself compelled to argue the case against anything other than flat-rate subsidies. Any alternative to his own scheme would mean an appeals procedure with consequent delays to the all-important task of building houses to be let at rents which the men who built them could afford.

Houses to be built under his scheme would be eligible for subsidies of £9 per house per annum in urban areas, and £12 10s in rural parishes. Rate contributions were fixed at £4 10s as a maximum payable by local authorities on each house built. The subsidies were also to be available to private enterprise firms, but only on condition that they built houses to let at rents which did not exceed those charged by local authorities for similar houses. In effect, all houses built with the subsidy, whether by local authorities or for private enterprise, were to be for letting.

On this principle of building for letting, Wheatley would not shift his position, though his bill provided for a thorough review of subsidies paid out at the end of a three-year period of the scheme's operation. At times, he found himself under a cross-fire of demands from both sides of the industry. In late May, the National Federation of House Builders surprised him by calling for a state takeover of brickworks to ensure their co-operation with the scheme. 'They are more radical than I am', he minuted at this point, and he had to work hard to win the federation round to the belief that his scheme could operate on a voluntary basis.

Ten days after that he was faced with what could have been wrecking action by the bricklayers union, who threatened to withdraw over the issues of pay for 'wet time' and the admission of twenty-year-olds to apprenticeships. In this situation, and near to exhaustion, he secured the Prime Minister's intervention to talk delegates from the bricklayers' unions round to acceptance of the scheme.

After the bill's formal first reading, real debate began on the money resolutions which its subsidy provisions required to be laid before Parliament. This was his opportunity to take the Commons back through the various stages of the bill's preparations. Unions and employers in the building industry, he declared, had agreed to a treaty under his ministry's auspices to guarantee the industry's future by a suspension of the laws of supply and demand. Profiteering in bricks and other materials he admitted to be a problem, but assured the House of a separate bill in preparation to control this danger. This was in reply to the Liberal, Charles Masterman, who had praised the 'extraordinary lucidity and excellence' of the Minister's performance but quoted against him his own many attacks on price rings in the building industry 'which I regret to say he has now fallen a victim to in amorous relations'.[27]

Three weeks later the nine clauses and two schedules of the Housing (Financial Provisions) Bill went before the Commons for a full second reading debate. Once again, Wheatley impressed the House with a clear and able exposition of his case and the bill was carried by 315 votes to 175. Only 128 Conservatives went into the lobbies against the bill, but the danger ahead lay in the total of seventy-six amendments of which notice was given for its committee stage. Some of these could have buried the bill but for the developing relationship between Charles Masterman and Wheatley. The former's reliability in delivering a series of Liberal votes to defeat many destructive and unworkable amendments earned Wheatley's profound and expressed gratitude. Masterman's widow, Lucy, was not far wrong when she later wrote that her husband had 'carried Wheatley on his back'.[28]

In the end, sixty-six of the amendments were accepted by Wheatley. Some simply plugged gaps in the bill, like Neville Chamberlain's proposal that there be no sale of houses built under the bill without the Minister's consent and no subletting of the houses of tenants. An odd omission in the bill, that of a fair wage clause in building contracts under its terms, was also repaired by a Chamberlain amendment. On rents to be charged on houses built under its terms, the bill has been accused of vagueness. It sought to return to the principles of Addison's Act by fixing rents in relation to those of pre-war houses controlled by the 1915 scheme. These controlled rents, however, would only be a basis for the average rent each local authority might charge. This average rent was not to exceed the rents of similar controlled houses unless annual costs incurred by local authorities exceeded their rate contribution of £4 10s per annum per house. Local authorities were, thus, so long as they kept to these conditions, left to their own discretion as to what rent they would charge for individual houses.

Some of the strongest opposition to the bill's rental clauses came from Ernest Simon, Liberal MP for the Withington seat in Manchester. He had recently been Lord Mayor of Manchester and was, in the inter-war period, a considerable authority on housing. He claimed that the bill as it stood would allow local authorities to create a privileged class of tenants, and he moved an amendment to ensure that the rents of houses built under the bill must be the same as those for similar houses already existing in each relevant local authority area. Wheatley reacted to the insertion of any statutory requirement of this type as a way of pricing the houses his bill would provide out of reach of those for whom they were intended. He strongly rejected any suggestion of using existing commercially set rents as any sort of model for his bill. His arguments carried enough weight with Simon's fellow Liberals to bring most of them into the government lobby when the amendment was voted on and it was thrown out by a clear majority.

A further amendment by Simon would have introduced to the bill the principle of differential rents for tenants depending on whether or not they had children. A powerful intervention by the Attorney-General, Sir Patrick Hastings, who endorsed Wheatley's view that this would need for its enforcement an inquisitorial apparatus, ensured its decisive rejection. Simon, however, maintained his opposition, in speeches and in writing, to these aspects of the bill long after it came into operation.

Another defeated amendment was one moved by the Conservative, Walter Elliot, in order to introduce to the bill the principle of a definite quota of Scottish houses within the period in which the subsidies would operate. Wheatley had not ceased to be in sympathy with the case for Scottish self-government, but he argued strongly against Elliot that the bill should treat the United Kingdom as a unit. Nobody was less likely than he to deny Scotland's special housing problems but, he asked, would failure by local authorities to meet their quota under his bill mean financial penalties for them, and should quotas be set for different parts of England? Elliot's amendment was rejected by 231 votes to 139.

The wear and tear of long hours worked on the bill's preparation and on seeing it through Parliament made the strain on Wheatley quite visible and at times a matter of press comment. Prone as he was to weight and high blood pressure, there were times when those close to him feared he was driving himself to the limit, but he was in his place to move the bill's third reading on 25 July. The outcome of the debate was not in doubt, the bill getting its third reading by 226 votes to 131. Yet again Wheatley restated the philosophy behind his bill in a speech that underlined how he had set out to distance himself from the excitement of the Clydesiders' send-off from St Enoch's Station in order to steer through Parliament an attainable measure of real reform. 'Why did I not introduce a Socialist measure?', he asked the benches behind him as much as those opposite. 'I was not in a position to introduce a Socialist measure. The country is not ready for Socialism. I wish it were ready for it. I will devote my life to an honest effort to prepare it for Socialism. Meanwhile I have to take things as I find them.'[29]

Amongst the final speeches before the third reading division was a handsome tribute to Wheatley from Charles Masterman:

> For over six months with extraordinary patience and industry, with humour and a willingness to compromise and with all the arts of one who might have sat in the House for twenty years on the Front Bench, he has conducted a difficult bill in such a manner as to disarm opposition and he has always been ready to accept proposals which he knew would make the bill better.[30]

Masterman has also left us in the Liberal weekly the *Nation* a vivid description of Wheatley in action during this period:

> The House has found a new favourite in Mr Wheatley. He has been the one conspicuous success in the new Parliament. A short, squat middle-aged man with a chubby face beaming behind large spectacles, he trots about like a benign Pickwick, or a sympathetic country solicitor to whom the most reticent would be glad to confide the darkest secret. But he possesses a perfect Parlia-mentary manner; a pleasant voice, confident without arrogance, a quick power of repartee, a capacity for convincing statements, and above all, the saving grace of humour.[30]

If Wheatley was ready to resort to the 'soft word that turneth away wrath', it was to ease the passage of a bill to which he was deeply committed. The remainder of his few years in the House would show that, unmuzzled by office, he still had a cutting-edge that could make him a formidable and sometimes ruthless opponent.

In the Lords, the principle of subsidised rents came under attack from what he at once identified as a 'wrecking amendment' which sought to base the rents for houses built under Wheatley's scheme on those charged to tenants of 'uncontrolled' pre-war houses. Wheatley made it clear that he would sacrifice the whole bill rather than give way over this and the Lords backed down. He did, however, accept an amendment from them, which he added to the bill as a tenth clause, to the effect that houses under the bill could be built with materials other than bricks. One supporter of this change was Lord Weir, owner of the Cathcart engineering works and fierce wartime opponent of the Clyde Workers Committee. His company exploited this additional clause to build many controversial steel-frame houses, not just for sale but for local authorities under the 1924 bill once it became law. Weir claimed Wheatley had been privately sympathetic to this experiment, though not with any intention to use steel houses to break the power of the building unions, which was what Weir attempted to do.

The Housing (Financial Provisions) Bill received the Royal assent on 7 August, Parliament's last sitting day before the summer recess. Wheatley himself, after all the work he had put in to ensure the bill's passage, was not seen that day. John Scanlon later explained why:

> He had taken his usual bus to Whitehall and had decided to go to Victoria instead. He had looked at the noticeboard as to where trains were going, and had liked the name Littlehampton, without

having the remotest idea what it was like. He had walked out of Littlehampton station into a field, and lain down with his jacket under his head and his handkerchief over his face, and just slept.[32]

A good deal of the emphasis in recent writing by Ian MacLean, amongst others, has been placed on the shortcomings of the 1924 Housing Act. Wheatley had never claimed it to be a cure-all for Britain's housing problems, and it is sometimes forgotten that it was conceived by him as part of a dual strategy to accelerate the rate of local authority house-building. The second part of the strategy was the Building Materials Bill, which he prepared with as much care as the Housing Bill itself. The purpose of this legislation was to give the government sanctions against obstruction of its intentions by the suppliers of essential building materials. Talks with the suppliers and their representatives dragged on into late summer before a bill was ready for presentation to Parliament, and lobbying against some of its provisions continued on into the autumn of 1924.

Wheatley's patient work with the major materials supply firms was almost undone by an injudicious intervention by Hastings, the Attorney-General, who, in a speech to a Labour audience at Wallsend in July, celebrated the bill as one of the government's most clearly socialist measures. This was quite at variance with the low-key approach by Wheatley to steering through a bill that would be essential to the proper working of his Housing Act. The intentions of the bill were to give the government substantial powers to investigate and control prices and conditions which the suppliers attached to materials made available for contracts under the Act. In cases of proven and extreme profiteering, the bill provided a mechanism for the Ministry of Health to requisition material and take over the firms concerned, though in such cases compensation would be offered.

Opposition to these provisions slowed the bill's progress

through parliament, while a major strike by building workers in September put further pressure on Wheatley, since many building-site suppliers treated the strike as a good reason for holding back on the delivery of essential materials. As with the main Housing Bill, Wheatley made a virtue out of giving detailed consideration to all objections without compromising his fundamental aims, and the bill had still not completed its passage through Parliament when the government fell in October 1924. The loss of the bill deprived the government and its successors of control over a vital element in the cost of house construction. Wheatley's Housing Act was, thus, a weapon fated only to be used at half-cock, though in fact much was accomplished under its terms.

Under the 1924 Act, house-building went ahead at a pace which even its critics had to acknowledge. Thousands of building workers were brought back into employment under the Act and a record was set in 1927, when 273,000 houses were completed. 'A fine achievement', Simon later conceded, 'The biggest thing that has been done for housing and employment by any government.'[33] Only in that year did building under the Act begin to move into surplus over demand. Before that critics like Simon even argued that building had been too rapid, giving the building industry an artificial stimulus which could not last: 'The failure to use the great machine created at such cost by 1927 is nothing less than a tragedy of national planning.'[34] It was a failure which can hardly be blamed upon the architect of the 1924 Act, who was barely in office long enough to see it being brought into operation.

A more serious charge against the way the Act was operated was voiced by Simon: that it set a pattern of rents which largely excluded from its terms lower paid workers. Reports issued annually by the Department of Health for Scotland can be quoted to bear this out. In the period immediately after the

1924 bill became law, rents of houses built by local authorities under the scheme averaged around fifteen shillings per week and were much sought after. Yet the evidence suggests that Simon, within less than five years of the bill's enactment, was well justified in declaring, 'We shall have solved the housing problem of the clerk and the well-to-do artisan at a cost of something approaching £10,000,000 a year. The slums will be almost untouched, and we shall have done nothing for the poorest families.'[35]

The loss of the Building Materials Bill, it needs to be repeated, removed a potentially important means to lower rents by keeping upper limits to the prices suppliers could charge local housing authorities. Wheatley's speeches and writings on housing make it clear that he never deceived himself into thinking that his Act could solve the housing problem, least of all with the Conservatives back in power and only a minority of local councils under Labour control. Subsidies payable under the scheme were, moreover, reduced by Chamberlain in 1928 (though reinstated a year later by the second Labour government). Towards the end of the Act's life, and after Wheatley's own death, a fall in building costs and in interest rates was, in fact, allowing more houses at lower rents to be built, only for the Act to be repealed by the National government in 1932.

It is, therefore, a rather specious argument to call Wheatley's housing policy merely 'a continuation of Neville Chamberlain's',[36] given that governments in which the latter figured prominently cut subsidies under the 1924 Act and then repealed it altogether. True, the Chamberlain Act of 1923, like Addison's 1919 Act, rested on the principle of subsidised house-building, and schemes were still going ahead under these Acts, particularly Chamberlain's at the moment of the 1924 government's resignation, for local authorities needed time to draw up plans for building under the terms of the Wheatley

Act. Wheatley, indeed, was careful to stress in the Commons that there was no necessary incompatibility'[37] between his legislation and Chamberlain's.

In the implementation of Wheatley's Act much depended on the politics of local government. In Glasgow a strong labour movement, though not able to take control of the city until 1933 after the Wheatley Act was repealed, was able to push hard for priority to be given to building schemes under its terms. Wheatley's work was certainly the most important factor in Glasgow housing expansion between the wars. Over 21,500 two- and three-apartment houses, many with garden access at ground-floor level, were built under his Act. This was almost 42 per cent of all houses built with government assistance in the inter-war period. None of these houses was built at a height of more than three storeys, and few schemes completed under the 1924 Act have became social disaster areas comparable to some of the results of later high-rise developments in Glasgow and elsewhere.

Much criticism of Wheatley's work on housing is based on charges that he failed to solve problems which he never claimed his legislation would attack, least of all in the hands of Conservative successors to a short-lived minority Labour government. The suggestion has been made, too, that in departmental terms he was an 'ideal' minister who would never stray from a civil service brief. This was not the view of many who observed Wheatley in action during his nine months in office. To some of them the difference was apparent in the second Labour government in which Wheatley declined to serve. Writing of the Housing Ministry's lack of direction under Greenwood in 1929, E. D. Simon wrote: 'I assume that it must have been partly due to the fact that the Minister of Health (especially in a Labour Government) is a very hardworked and overburdened man, and partly to the official and cautious atmosphere of the Ministry which, though it failed to affect Mr Wheatley's views and energy, seemed completely to capture Mr Greenwood.'[38]

Wheatley, it must be stressed again, took office unburdened by illusions about what he or the Labour government itself could achieve. 'Housing reform', he later declared, 'is the red cross work of the class struggle.' It was rescue work which cried out to be done, in his own Shettleston constituency and over the length and breadth of Britain. A grateful generation who were able to move into 'Wheatley houses' did not forget a minister who had staked everything on the belief that market forces alone could never meet one of the most basic human needs.

'On matters of health we are all Socialists now',[39] he had told the Imperial Social Hygiene Congress in May 1924, but this claim was, in the minds of many in the labour movement, called in question by his handling of the question of birth control. This was the issue over which he drew most attack on himself from within the labour movement during his time in office. It is perhaps the one clear instance in Wheatley's political career when his allegiance to the teaching of his church took precedence over any other considerations. A birth-control lobby was strong and vocal by 1924, its hand strengthened by a controversial prosecution the year before for selling a leaflet on the subject of the Glasgow anarchist, Guy Aldred, and his companion and mother of his child, Rose Witcop.

Before January 1924, Ministry of Health policy on the matter was clear enough: it forbade doctors or health visitors to give advice on contraception, and, indeed, reserved the right to withdraw funding of health centres known by it to give such advice. The hope that Wheatley might alter the Ministry's policy prompted a powerful deputation representing the birth-control lobby to meet him early in May. It was led by Bertrand

Russell's wife, Dora, and included H. G. Wells, Francis Huxley and others active in the campaign to make basic contraceptive knowledge widely available.

It is difficult to think that the deputation expected any other reply than it got, which was that in Wheatley's view 'state and rate-aided institutions could not, on such a matter, be permitted to give this advice by mere administrative action – the authority of Parliament was necessary'.[40] What angered the campaign more than this was the rest of Wheatley's answer, based, it would seem, on a departmental brief, that 'where contraception was necessary on strict medical grounds, the patient must go to a private doctor or hospital'.[41] 'Mr Wheatley had stirred a hornet's nest: all through 1924 we buzzed and stung',[42] Dora Russell wrote later. He was, indeed, vulnerable to attack on several fronts, as the professional medical press shows, for there his willingness to refer women for birth-control advice to private hospitals or doctors was interpreted as his pre-empting recommendations which doctors might make. By no means all private hospitals were equipped to provide such information anyhow, while reliance on private medicine sat uneasily with his clearly stated socialist convictions on other health matters. Dora Russell attacked him strongly in reply to speeches he made during a National Baby Week in July, and the hostile questioning began to require his presence in Parliament to defend his ministry's position.

To the English Speaking Conference on Infant Welfare at its Caxton Hall conference in July, he spoke on motherhood without reference to the controversy over which he was under attack. 'Their duty', he told delegates, including many women, 'was not to relieve the mothers of their functions and duties, but rather to train and help them to perform them satisfactorily',[43] and his speech was taken up mainly with the education and training of mothers and the expansion of welfare and midwifery services. The matter of a woman's choice as to whether and when to have children was predictably absent from his text.

His replies to questions in Parliament showed little movement from his response to the May deputation, though some members tried to put him under pressure by stressing the relationship between an absence of adequate contraceptive knowledge and the increase in abortion. Criticism of his stance was firmly endorsed by the Labour Women's Conference in late May, but little more could be drawn from him than that which he had already offered. To another deputation in August of the Standing Joint Committee of Women's Industrial Organizations, he presented the issue as 'whether birth control was desirable, and whether or not it should be taught in a particular place or manner'.[44] He stressed the controversial nature of the question and the degree to which the working class was disunited over it: 'Women might have reasons [on which he did not elaborate] other than religious objections for not attending centres authorized to give birth-control advice.'[45]

He clearly felt little option but to shield himself behind the contention that new legislation must be a precondition of birth-control advice being given in health centres and clinics. Membership of a minority government with a full legislative programme gave him a pretext for avoiding any decision, as did his belief in the angry controversy that would be likely to confront a Catholic minister from his background making any concessions to a practice that church teaching still condemned unequivocally. His response falls far short of what, by today's standards, we may think it ought to have been, and indeed from that of continental Social Democratic parties to the issue. Two years later, though, a Labour conference censured the National Executive Committee for averting a birth-control debate. The censure motion was carried by only the barest of majorities.

Catholicism as a movement within the labour movement was a force which would long outlive Wheatley himself.

Even before the fall of the Labour government, Wheatley was making some attempt to evaluate his experience in it in relation to some of the broader issues he had confronted in his debates the year before with Brailsford and others over Labour's international policy and in his pamphlet *Starving in the Midst of Plenty*. Mounting capitalist crisis could, in his view, expedite a British transition to socialism, but this transition could not be achieved amidst mass working-class poverty. It depended, on the contrary, on carefully thought out measures to end the chronic under-consumption which was a permanent brake upon the economy's growth.

The economy he was talking about was the British economy, and the apparatus for its regeneration would be provided by the British state and by developing Britain's relationship to its overseas dominions. Wheatley, at Johnston's suggestion, had joined the Commonwealth Labour group of MPs formed when he entered the House in 1922, and its chairman, L. Haden Guest, was one of his Parliamentary Private Secretaries during his ministerial term. 'We must learn', he wrote in 1924, 'to think of Imperial affairs as being really Home affairs. The British Empire will be very soon as close and compact as Britain itself was a century ago',[46] and he looked to the labour movement in Britain and the dominions to guarantee that this link would be made. The racist white labour policy of a labour movement like that in Australia was something of which he was either unaware or which he ignored.

He did, however, agree to act well outside his ministerial remit by presenting to the full cabinet the Commonwealth group's views on the future of India. These were based on the belief that in any free British Commonwealth of Nations worthy of the name, India should take its part as a self-governing partner within an agreed timetable. With the government near-ing the end of its tenure, Wheatley submitted to his colleagues a memorandum based on the group's views, which received predictably short shrift.

That British economic recovery could be achieved, he re-mained confident, even as he realised how the government in which he had taken part lacked a strategy to bring it about.

> A general increase in the purchasing power of the people can be brought about only through national organization. . . Under the system of a national pool, nationally controlled (which might in our case become an Empire pool) industries that are now neglect-ed, because they provide no national profit, could be worked to the common benefit as part of a national scheme.[47]

National efficiency within a 'greater Britain' linked to its dominion partners as the way to socialist advance was a far cry from the cause of Irish self-determination which had first brought Wheatley into politics; and where did it leave his com-mitment to what was still Labour's policy of Scottish Home Rule? The priority he would have given to this had he been made Secretary of State for Scotland instead of Health Minister can be a matter only of speculation. While in office in 1924 he certainly remained in contact with the all-party Scottish Home Rule Association, which, over the previous year or two, had organised, with prominent Labour support, some of the biggest political demonstrations in Scotland. The 1924 government made no time, however, even for a token attempt at Home Rule legislation, and Wheatley, under the constraints imposed by office, took no part in the May debate which led to George Buchannan's Private Members bill for a system of federal Home Rule being talked out by Conservative opponents. At the very moment of the government's fall, however, he was willing to be quoted unofficially as a supporter of the calling of a Scottish convention on self-government and was a backer of a

later attempt by Labour members (in 1928) to push Home
Rule legislation through Parliament. The cause was not one on
which any Labour government attempted seriously to legislate
for another fifty years, though it should not be dismissed merely
as 'a piece of old radical baggage which the Clydesiders and
others carried through to an age in which it no longer held
their clothes'.[48]

People who saw anything of Wheatley outside cabinet and
House of Commons hours doubted whether he had really taken
to a minister's routine, with the numerous receptions and official social gatherings it required. At times, escape from it was
a necessity, as Gallacher recalled later:

> One evening, when he had accompanied me to an open-air meet-
> ing in Finsbury Park, we got a bus back to the Angel and went
> into a Lyons cafe for tea and buns. John was pleased with the
> meeting; it had been like a breath of fresh air after all he had to
> go through with these abortive Cabinet meetings. 'You know,
> Willie', he said, 'it made me feel that I was back home in
> Glasgow.'[49]

Wheatley's continued contact with Gallacher is interesting
because in April he had agreed to serve on a five-man cabinet
committee on industrial unrest and the extent of supposed
communist influence upon it. This committee reported in May
that such influence was, in fact, very limited and that the
Communist Party had serious problems over its membership
and finances. Nonetheless, it had clearly used evidence supplied
by the Special Branch and MI5 who were engaged in the
surveillance of activists like Gallacher. Its creation, and its
report, it has been said, 'marked a turning point in Labour's
relationship with the intelligence services'.[50] If so, Wheatley
did not let it get in the way of a relationship with Gallacher
that went back ten years at least, and he may well have been
struck by the irony of the government later, in October,

falling victim to the readiness of Fleet Street and the Conservatives to make political use of a Comintern document against it in a general election.

By the late summer of 1924 Wheatley was visibly a tired man and, increasingly, he was isolated from the cabinet as a whole. He formed no alliances within it to offset a deterioration in relations with MacDonald which dated back at least to the circumstances of his appointment to the cabinet and which his handling of the Poplar controversy had not improved. He was unhappy, too, at the orthodoxy of Snowden's Budget and came to feel that, even with a parliamentary majority behind it, the cabinet under MacDonald's leadership would not come up with any radical strategy to tackle slump and unemployment. Some of those close to Wheatley, like Scanlon, were of the opinion that he was contemplating resignation anyhow once his housing legislation had become law. Their belief was not put to the test because of the government's inept handling of the Campbell case in October. MacDonald was already under attack for his policy of reopening commercial and political relations with Russia when the decision was taken to call off the prosecution of the communist, J. R. Campbell, on charges of incitement to mutiny in the armed forces.

The cabinet split over how much of the responsibility should be laid upon Sir Patrick Hastings, the Attorney-General. Wheatley was among those who protested at a colleague being used to extricate the government from mounting embarrassment: 'I strongly object', he declared, 'to Hastings being sacrificed to save MacDonald's face.' Indeed, he seems to have been ready to resign with Hastings if need be. Neither his resignation nor that of Hastings was required, however, thanks to the Liberals' tactic of moving for a Select Committee on the whole matter. Wheatley appears, on the basis of a conversation which Masterman later recalled, to have thought it would be enough for the government to accept the Select Committee. The Liberal move could have kept the Labour government in office, but the government chose to equate their call for a Select Committee with the Conservatives' censure motion and resigned on 9 October after this response had produced a Conservative–Liberal alliance in a crucial Commons vote.

8 Opposition and another Labour government

I

The 1924 election produced for Labour an overall loss of forty seats but a gain of 1 million additional votes, partly because many more seats were contested. MacDonald let himself be forced onto the defensive by the leaking in the *Daily Mail* of the Zinoviev letter alleging planned communist infiltration of the British armed forces. Labour candidates had to counter as best they could the scare-mongering tactics of opponents who were not fastidious about the accusations they made. Shifting attention from the Zinoviev scare and the labour movement's alleged affinities with the USSR back to actual policy issues proved a losing battle in all too many constituencies, but Wheatley's efforts gave encouragement to many other Labour candidates.

He, of course, had his own Housing Act to defend, and he wrote the preface to an election pamphlet, Labour Solves the Housing Problem, as well as devoting many speeches to explaining in detail how subsidies would work under the new legislation. His campaign went beyond putting the case for what he admitted were Labour's achievements in office to drawing lessons from the experience. It had, he told one election audience, posed a choice which could not be much longer deferred between the waste and failure of competitive capitalism and a rational mobilisation of the community's skills to provide for the needs of all. Labour's opponents, he declared, feared the new society which would be born despite them: 'They stand trembling on the shore as the early man must have stood before he built his first canoe.'[1] In other speeches and articles he reverted to the analysis of capitalism which, under Hobson's influence, he had been developing before joining the Labour government. 'British capitalism', he conceded, 'like other criminals, had a virtuous youth. It performed some useful service. The pioneers, like Stevenson, Watt and Bell, enabled it to produce wealth at a rate unknown before',[2] but, he argued, the surplus it had created in its dynamic phase was now largely investment capital exported abroad, existing in a parasitic relationship to the needs of industry as well as contributing to a further reduction in levels of consumption at home.

As to the Zinoviev letter, he poured scorn on it as a typical concoction of the capitalist press to discredit both Labour and the USSR, a great country undergoing a dramatic transition which Britain should support. On the Campbell case, which had brought down the Labour government, he denied the accusations made by leading Conservative speakers and by Lloyd George that he personally had wrecked an eleventh-hour Labour *rapprochement* with the Liberals. He was emphatic that the government's decision to go had been a unanimous one, but he alarmed the Labour leadership by the tone of his support for the communist, J. R. Campbell. Open recourse by the capitalist state to the armed forces to crush Labour was not far away, he told a Dumbarton audience, adding that 'if Campbell is a criminal for his view of the workers' right to resist the military then so am I'.[3]

With the final results of the election clear, Wheatley drew solace from defeat, representing it as a new threshold of socialist opportunity after the necessary but frustrating compromises of minority government:

Labour is freed from a difficult position. We can now return to a fighting policy. It is clear that a timid, statesman-like attitude makes no appeal to a people struggling to emancipate themselves from poverty. The points of attack should now be mainly domestic.[4]

The Wheatley of the 1924 election cut a strikingly different figure from the fastidious parliamentary tactician of a few months before, steering complex legislation through the House with a skill that won cross-bench respect. His election speeches and writings had a cutting and militant edge to them that goaded his Conservative opponent in Shettleston into increasingly bitter attacks. This was W. Reid Miller, a businessman with connections to the Orange Order, who had no hesitation in attacking Wheatley for his Irish origins and his Catholicism, or in spreading rumours about his business interests.

Hostility to Wheatley for his Catholicism was not confined to Conservatives. The private papers of J. Walton Newbold, communist MP for Motherwell from 1922 to 1924 who subsequently joined the Labour Party, drip with malice against Wheatley for his allegedly Jesuitical capacity for intrigue and his ability to influence colleagues like Maxton on issues such as birth control. The 1924 contest is perhaps the first clear sign of an increasingly strident anti-Catholicism which disfigured much of Scottish life in the inter-war period. Wheatley was not the only victim, though he held his seat in Shettleston with the slender majority of 630 votes. Ironically, he was also the target of attack from the local Catholic press. The *Glasgow Observer*'s support for Labour, which had developed since the end of the war and the demise of the old United Irish League, was becoming increasingly selective. Its editor parodied Wheatley's speeches analysing capitalism's inherent weaknesses: 'Meantime, we believe the business of which he is the chief proprietor is carried on just as usual.'[5] The *Observer* returned to the attack the following year with increased venom: 'Wheatley has held office and has been as cunning as he is insinuating in his conduct since he was first returned to Parliament as a Labour Member. The ILP is still within the party and it is just as objectionable in its ways as are the Communists. In fact the ILP *is* practically a Communist party.'⁶ Earlier in the year it quoted Wheatley on the ruthlessness of much business practice and declared, 'he talks with a double tongue on social, political, and economic questions. We say that Mr Wheatley in his own affairs displays all those characteristics of capitalism and all those harsh methods.'⁷ The more damaging of this cross-fire was that maintained by Reid Miller despite his failure to unseat Wheatley in 1924. Wheatley continued to be a major figure on the national political stage, but the defence of his personal and business integrity became an increasing preoccupation which would almost lead to his premature departure from politics.

In the new Parliament which opened in 1925, Wheatley continued to speak frequently on housing policy, reiterating the case for his own Act and stressing the virtues of his aborted Building Materials Bill, which would have kept a brake on building costs. He attacked Lord Weir, the industrialist and old enemy of the Clydesiders in wartime, for exploiting an amendment that Wheatley had accepted to the 1924 Act to allow the use of alternative materials in house construction. Firms controlled by Weir were building steel houses under the Act, often with labour paid well under accepted union rates. The size of houses being built under his scheme was being reduced, too, he pointed out in several speeches. Labour in office had ensured that 75 per cent of all houses in plans submitted to the Scottish Board of Health had two rooms or more. By August of 1925 he was able to show parliament that the figure had slipped to 60 per cent.

Wheatley remained preoccupied with the lessons to be learnt from Labour's short experience of office and was open to argument about the direction which the movement should commit itself in opposition. He kept in touch with Gallacher until the latter, with other leading communists, was arrested on conspiracy and incitement charges late in 1925. Gallacher seems to have found the relationship frustrating and claimed later in his memoirs that Wheatley held back from agreeing to make any real bid for support from the constituency parties in order to challenge the drift of leadership policy. He was fearful, too, in Gallacher's recollection, of being openly associated with communist aims, despite his readiness to support Maxton on the issue of communists having the right to Labour Party membership.

That it had been office, rather than power, which he and his cabinet colleagues had exercised, emerged with growing conviction in his contributions to the debate about Labour's experience in government. In April 1925, for example, at the ILP's annual conference, he seconded a resolution moved by Kirkwood which was based upon the failure of capitalism and the need for bold socialist measures from any subsequent Labour government. In his speech Wheatley drew upon his own recent ministerial experience to range beyond the motion itself:

> Labour should not again accept office as a minority. If Labour went back as a minority Government, it went back to administer a capitalist order of society that would only bring discredit to the party. The ILP should organize itself increasingly to bring a united working class. Let us fight every day to overthrow the capitalist order of society in which we no longer believe.[8]

At this same conference Wheatley was elected, with Maxton amongst others, to membership of the new ILP Parliamentary Committee. He was already on the party's National Administrative Council, though he had been irregular in his attendance during his months as minister. Strategically, he was thus well placed within the ILP to develop both his critique of capitalism and what the Labour movement's policy priorities should be. His continuing commitment to the ILP was important too, because the experience of government had done little for its relationships to the Labour leadership.

Over much of Britain, the ILP was still the Labour Party for many people, and determined activism within it could, if coupled with ambition and a capacity for oratory, promote individual careers with a rapidity which sometimes made for cynicism. A case in point was Oswald Mosley, with whom for a time Wheatley's political fortunes overlapped. After Mosley resigned his seat in Parliament in 1924 to join the ILP, offers of adoption as a candidate in winable Labour seats poured in and it was the ILP's Glasgow Federation which was instrumental in waiving party rules to enable him to become a candidate as quickly as he did.

On several occasions before and after his return to Parliament in 1926, Wheatley shared platforms with Mosley and took the chair for him on other occasions in Glasgow; they were also guest speakers together at ILP Summer Schools. No two men could have been less alike in background, appearance or political style, yet it is clear that Mosley thought highly of Wheatley. Writing of him many years later in his memoirs, Mosley described him as

> the most remarkable man among the Clydesiders, the only man of Lenin quality that the English [sic] left has ever produced. His method in debate was cold, incisive, steely and contrasted completely with the emotionalism of his colleagues, particularly Maxton. Wheatley was a master of facts and figures, and far more than any other member of the Labour Party, impressed me as a man who might get things done: it followed naturally that MacDonald detested him.[9]

What drew Wheatley and Mosley quite close to each other

was the reality of Britain's post-war economic crisis. Central to this crisis was, of course, an intractable level of unemployment which mocked the hopes of returned soldiers and the promises of politicians. The consensus of expert opinion saw this unemployment as a product of temporary dislocations, caused by the war, to world trade and to the monetary system. The remedy was seen to lie in the recovery of lost markets, cutting costs and restoring stability to the world's exchange rates. This last objective, it was widely believed, required Britain's return to the gold standard at pre-war parity.

Between 1922 and 1930 Wheatley and Mosley shared what was, at times, an equal prominence in their campaign against this consensus, although later historians have tended to emphasise the role of Mosley rather than of Wheatley. J. A. Hobson's under-consumptionist analysis of capitalism's failure and its influence upon Wheatley has already been mentioned. Hobson had developed this theory quite extensively by the time of Wheatley's entry into parliament, and in 1922 produced a book, *The Economics of Unemployment,* which was much discussed in *Forward* and the *New Leader.* Many of Wheatley's early speeches in Parliament were clearly Hobsonian in their content; Keynesian economics, it has sometimes been claimed, owed much to Hobson, and Keynes in his 1923 *Tract for Monetary Reform* did make a frontal attack on those in the Bank of England and the Treasury who were pushing the case for deflation.

Deflationary policies, Keynes argued, were the product of particular interest groups, involving the transfer of real wealth and spending power away from the community's most productive part to its inactive *rentier* element. However, Keynes presented his case in such a way as to assume an identity of interest between workers and manufacturers against their common enemy, the bankers and *rentiers.* Marxists have always been critical of Keynes for the limits of his perception of class struggle under capitalism, as well as for the priority he gave to cheap money and government-funded economic growth over actual income redistribution; and Wheatley certainly shared many of these reservations.

Wheatley and Mosley were attracted, for different reasons, to a modified view of under-consumptionist theory. For Wheatley, with his background in Catholic social thought, the idea of a community of interest between industrial employers and workers in opposition to banks and financiers commended itself, at least temporarily. In the Commons for example, in April 1925, he called for an end to economic civil war: 'We as a nation sink or swim together. . . the industrialists of this country will be driven sooner or later to take up arms against the financiers and to apply the principles of Socialism in advance in order to save their industries'.[10] A year later, once the General Strike was called, such a community of interest would be less apparent.

Later in 1925 Wheatley supported Mosley's Birmingham programme with its call for an incomes policy, state management of credit through control of the banks, abandonment of the gold standard and a national corporation to plan output in key industries. Absent from these proposals was any commitment to income redistribution through taxation, something Wheatley never surrendered his belief in as a means to revive demand in the economy and reduce inequality. An emphasis on the shared objectives of masters and men was central to the increasingly corporatist thrust of Mosley's thinking which would soon take him out of the labour movement. That was a road along which Wheatley was never tempted to travel.

He gave his most committed support to the ILP document 'The Living Wage', produced the following year by a study group set up by the party chairman, Allen, which included,

among others, J. A. Hobson and H. N. Brailsford. Its economic analysis was, in essence, under-consumptionist, and while it
accepted the principle of public ownership of major industries,
this was subordinated to the revival of working-class purchasing
power through (amongst other measures) a family allowance
scheme to be funded from taxation. As Robert Skidelsky has
pointed out, the emphasis was on fiscal policy, though the
authors recognised the limits of tax yield in a depressed economy, while Mosley's priorities were with monetary policy.[11]
Converted into the policy statement 'Socialism in Our Time',
these proposals were endorsed with enthusiasm at the ILP's
April 1926 Conference at Whitley Bay. In the debate Wheatley
urged upon delegates the view that there was no need for
socialists to wait until industries were nationalised before bringing about a significant redistribution of income.[12] Satisfaction at
the result of the conference was, however, quickly overtaken
by the drama of the General Strike.

Wheatley predicted the onset of the strike a good many
months before it happened, and gave unswerving support both
to the miners and to the TUC General Council's call to action
in solidarity with them. There was still a good deal of mining
in and near his own Shettleston constituency, so the business of
fund-raising, organising food and using all his own influence
and the ILP's resources had the most local and personal imme-
diacy for him. He contributed generously, donating his own
parliamentary salary to the support of the strike, and was
enraged at what he saw as the TUC's desertion of the miners
and the Labour leadership's meanness of spirit towards them.
He wrote at the end of May 1926:

> From the first moment of the struggle and indeed before it,
> prominent Labour leaders were whining and grovelling. Some,
> instead of going out to proclaim the justice of the workers' cause,
> spent their time damping the ardour of the courageous by wring-

161

ing their hands and talking about a tragedy. The real tragedy was that in its hour of trial the labour movement was deserted by those in whom it had placed its greatest trust.[13]

As the privations of the miners and their families worsened during the great lock-out, Wheatley marvelled at their capacity to endure suffering:

> If the endurance and determination they displayed had been on the battlefield on behalf of our ruling class and the prevailing order of society, their struggle would be the central feature in the history books of our schools for centuries to come. As it is, they are blackguarded for their bravery. We can never hope to see a better workers' fight again. Is there another million such men in this country?[14]

These comments were made by Wheatley as the resistance itself was beginning to crumble in many coalfields. Politically, the passion of his support for it had widened further the already existing gap between him and the Labour leadership, while some of his more militant utterances in the strike's earlier stages would be savoured by Unionist opponents in Glasgow, who wished for nothing better than to drive him out of public life for good.

More important for what remained of his political lifetime was Wheatley's readiness to come to terms with the significance of the way both the TUC and the miners had been defeated. The superhuman efforts of the miners could, he accepted, be asked of no other group within the labour force: 'Reviewing the matter calmly, I cannot see how a General Strike, constitutionally conducted, can attain its object. To be successful it would require to be swift and complete and backed by unconditional action.'[15] This assessment was not shared by others close to him at this time in the ILP like Maxton, Fenner Brockway and John Paton, who saw events since May as a heroic vindication of working-class solidarity and a preparation for fresh challenges to a capitalism in deepening crisis.

While the miners were still locked-out by the coal companies, Brailsford resigned his editorship of the *New Leader* after four years in which he had put his enormous energy and talent into transforming it into a highly successful paper. He had recruited Wheatley to its board and his biographer stresses the affinity between their views on many issues of the day while suggesting that Wheatley's Catholicism was a barrier to a personal friendship, given Brailsford's strongly agnostic views.[16] Allen's removal from the chairmanship of the ILP at the end of 1925 was blamed by Brailsford on an intrigue against him by Maxton and Wheatley, and this undermined his position as editor. After his departure, the economic analysis he had popularised with Hobson continued to be given space in the *New Leader*'s pages, and Wheatley himself remained a regular contributor until his death.

The breakup of the miners' solidarity also coincided with the annual Labour Conference in October 1926, at which the statement 'Socialism in Our Time', based on the 'Living Wage' document, was tabled for debate. Wheatley had strongly supported it at the ILP's 1926 Conference in April, though not all the party's divisional councils had done so. The Labour Conference, however, neutralised the document by referring it for further consideraiton to the National Executive after MacDonald had castigated it for its 'flashy futilities'. The ILP was not strongly enough entrenched at the conference, especially among the union delegations, to prevent this outcome, but a party commission was set up to study the ILP's recommendations and to report on them.

The conference debate on 'Socialism in Our Time' finished without Wheatley being called to speak. Angry scenes accompanied an abortive attempt by ILP delegates to have Standing Orders suspended so that he could be heard. In a real sense, this outcome was irrelevant, for in David Marquand's words, the ILP document 'mattered less as a programme than as a weapon in a struggle for power'.[17] It was a struggle which the ILP was no longer equipped to win, if indeed it ever had been. Membership was past its peak in 1928 and was starting to dwindle after Clifford Allen's energetic chairmanship, while the decision of Attlee, Charles Trevelyan and others to transfer their parliamentary candidatures to their divisional Labour parties pointed to a shedding of the middle-class element that had been influential within its counsels since the war.

In Scotland, however, the ILP remained a force even as this overall decline set in. In 1925 almost one-third of all its branches in Britain were in Scotland and new ones were still being formed. Wheatley's membership was something it could continue to take for granted, but the ILP was in no real sense a power base for him. In large part this was due to the growing influence of Dollan. At the party's Divisional Council meetings and conferences in Scotland, Dollan more often than not could use his influence to neutralise challenges to Labour's leadership launched by either Maxton or Wheatley. As John Paton put it, 'the prophets were without honour in their own country'.[18]

Wheatley could still hope to make an impact through his journalism or his speeches in Parliament. In the 1926 session he helped to orchestrate a protracted campaign against government legislation to effect economies in the administration and payment of unemployment benefit. Ultimately this campaign resorted to procedural obstruction in the Chamber and out of it. In April 1926 Wheatley and Lansbury led a group of another eleven Labour members who either sat or lay down on the floor of the division lobby to slow down voting on some of the amendments to the government scheme.

He kept working hard, moreover, to press the case for ideas broadly akin to those of ILP policy documents like 'Socialism in Our Time. In December 1928 he contributed three major articles to the *New Leader* on the theme of 'Why Capitalism is Failing'. These mapped out ground which Wheatley had already occupied in debates within the labour movement but are still an important and perhaps definitive insight into his thinking on the sort of economic policy that it was realistic for Labour to offer the electorate.

The first article, 'Why Capitalism is Failing', broke no new ground, simply reiterating under-consumptionist theory. The second, 'Treat Britain as One National Workshop', presented Wheatley's answers to those who called for cost-cutting and deflation as the key to making British industry competitive once more. The ultimate logic of this argument, he declared, was that 'the wages in our exporting industries, if fixed by competition, must be controlled by the lowest wages paid for similar work in any part of the world. The skilful savage will determine the living condition of civilized British workers.'[19] In place of this, he called for recognition of the interdependence of all industries and services which constituted the British economy: 'The capacity of the nation as a whole, and not of what we now call an industry, will determine wages. We must stifle the parrot cry that each industry must "face its economic facts", even to the extent of suicide.'[20]

Public ownership of key industries, he argued in his third and final article, 'A British Road to Socialism', was probably incompatible with a competitive wage system. State regulation of wages and prices was a precondition for nationalised industries and services to function rationally in a system which would both reward merit and maintain consumer demand at a level required for full employment. All three articles were shortly published as a leaflet, *Socialize the National Income!*, and served to distance Wheatley even further from the Labour leadership, but also from a socialist tradition that accorded workers an active role in managing their own industries and shaping state policy through their unions.

Wheatley's proposals still seem to presuppose a benign and creative role for the British state, and he made no demand for the restructuring of its institutions before this role was asked of it. Control of wages and prices, he argued, would be the work of a vaguely defined group of state 'directors', in whose selection all workers would 'have a voice'. He made no mention, however, of this voice being heard through the unions. In fact, there was no reference at all to what their function might be within a rejuvenated economy planned and run as a single 'national workshop'. The omission was a strange one given that elsewhere in the pamphlet he had stressed the transparent inequality under capitalism of servile wage-labour and autocratic employers.

In *Socialize the National Income!* Wheatley did address himself to the reality of a global capitalism which, increasingly, could play off against each other workers of different cultures and continents, and he reiterated his rejection of the internationalist and essentially Free Trade orthodoxies to which some Labour leaders still clung. Taken as a whole, however, the pamphlet can be seen as part of Wheatley's continuing search for answers which the existing British state under socialist control could provide to British problems.

This apparent lack of any receptiveness to the case for internationally based action to deal with a crisis of capitalism which went far beyond Britain in its effect has exposed Wheatley to criticism by Labour historians, as has the language he used about savages and coolies undercutting 'civilised' British workers' wages and conditions. At the very least, the terms in which he wrote of non-European peoples could sometimes be paternalist and dismissive enough to make for uneasy reading now. He was by no means unique in this, in the labour movement or outside it, and he did at least identify himself with the general thrust of Labour's imperial policy, which was one of economic co-operation with the white self-governing dominions and guided progress to autonomy for non-white peoples under British rule. To this extent Wheatley, with his votes for Imperial Preference and his disinclination to think in terms of European or international answers to capitalist crises, did adopt a broadly 'Labour imperialist' position. This was at odds with the analysis of H. N. Brailsford for one, who made a number of attacks upon Wheatley's views during his time as editor of the *New Leader*.

Wheatley's faith in what a planned and self-sufficient British economy could accomplish has been described as a non-Stalinist version of 'Socialism in One Country'. He never got the chance to visit the USSR but kept an active interest in policy debates there after Lenin's death, and in numerous speeches and articles he took an optimistic view of its initiatives in state economic planning. Such affirmative feelings for the USSR as Wheatley had expressed made little difference to an assessment of him written in 1926 by Trotsky. In a chapter of *Where is Britain Going?*, Trotsky flayed British Labour leaders for their commitment to the constraints of the parliamentary road. Wheatley did not escape, for his Catholicism made him a particularly tempting target:

> For this left-winger, Socialist policy is directed by personal morality and personal morality by religion. In no respect does this differ from Lloyd George who regards the church as the central electric station of all parties. Compromise here receives its religious sanctification.[21]

Despite Trotsky's caustic dismissal of his role, a gap was opening between Wheatley and a Labour leadership committed to a return to office with or without an overall majority. This gap was inseparable from the development of the ILP itself as a source of alternative socialist strategies. G. D. H. Cole identified this in a 1928 article in which he declared that

> the ILP has pretty clearly reached a point where it is trying to decide whether to dissolve its identity, in so far as policy is concerned, in a Labour Party which has outgrown its control, or to become a 'ginger group' within the larger party, consisting of persons who take the distinctly more radical view than the majority of its leaders.[22]

The year 1927 found Wheatley moving closer still to those who were in revolt against the direction of party policy under MacDonald. In March he left the opposition front bench and at the ILP's Leicester Conference threw his support behind the party's move to withdraw its nomination of MacDonald as Labour Party Treasurer. Personal preoccupations, however, intervened with dramatic effect to remove him for some months from the national political stage, and, indeed, almost to end his political career.

II

Wheatley's Unionist opponent in 1924, Reid Miller, having come as close as he did to winning the Shettleston seat, had kept up the offensive that had characterised his election campaign. He continued to attack at every opportunity Wheatley's Catholicism and Irish origins, but also directed his fire upon his business reputation. Amongst numerous allegations were claims that Wheatley was financially involved with money-lenders, publicans and building contractors. Miller also drew upon Wheatley's speeches and writings to suggest that he was a

Bolshevik sympathiser without respect for the oaths of allegiance to the Crown he had taken as an MP and Privy Councillor. To substantiate this last charge he claimed that Wheatley had been known to refuse to stand for the National Anthem at a local dinner. Many of these accusations were carried in the *Eastern Argus and Glasgow East End Advertizer*, a weekly paper owned by a business associate of Miller's, Alexander Anderson.

The *Catholic Herald*, it must be said, had also made serious allegations against Wheatley of a broadly similar nature, but Wheatley took no legal action against it. His decision to concentrate his fire upon a political opponent known to have connections with the Orange Order gave a sectarian cutting-edge to the events that followed. The opening shot in Wheatley's defence came in his own paper, the *Glasgow Eastern Standard* which, on 19 September 1925, printed a major article on Miller's allegations. This was entitled 'Mr Wheatley and his Traducers' and it offered £1,000, a large sum in 1925, to any person or persons who could provide evidence to bear out the charges being made. This challenge did little to reduce the venom with which the attack was maintained and fresh allegations against Wheatley came thick and fast.

These included the suggestion that those in Wheatley's employment were underpaid and exploited. This was ground already traversed earlier in the year during a strike by journalists employed at Hoxton and Walsh. They had full union representation and the matters at issue were settled, not without full publicity in the opposition press. Potentially most serious of all, however, was the accusation that Wheatley, while a minister in 1924, had used his influence to secure remission of heavy sentences for forgery passed upon two Shettleston Catholics, one of whom, James McVey, who was unemployed at the time of his conviction, lived near Wheatley's brother

Patrick. This allegation was never proved in open court, but in Miller's deposition it was linked to the Campbell case as proof of Wheatley's complicity in subverting the course of justice.

Wheatley's choice was either to ignore this accumulation of accusation and innuendo or to go to court against it. Protracted legal debates over the case developed after initial notice was served by Wheatley's lawyers of two actions against Miller and Anderson. These hinged upon the defendants' rights to have Wheatley's business affairs fully examined in open court and dragged on into the new year of 1927. The case finally went to trial before an Edinburgh jury in July 1927.

Wheatley sued each of his accusers for £3,000 on the ground that they had slandered him by malicious calumnies damaging to his personal and business reputation and likely to hold him up to public odium and contempt. The case required a very full examination of Wheatley himself, his brother Patrick, Thomas White, the solicitor who advised him on many business matters, and others who had at one time or another had financial interests in Hoxton and Walsh. One of these, also called James McVey, made no secret of his connections with the drink trade, but, like Wheatley himself and his brother Patrick, denied knowledge of ledgers and other documents which were felt by the court to be likely to clarify some of the major allegations.

It began to be clear to many following the case that there were indeed investors in Hoxton and Walsh, as there had been from the outset, with interests in the drink trade, something which did not compromise the integrity of Wheatley's own position on personal abstinence, but which did call in question the wisdom of a costly and increasingly bitter action. In the witness-box Wheatley himself had to admit to knowledge of a local joke in Shettleston centering on the request for 'a pint of Wheatley's' by customers in premises whose owners were known to have connections with Hoxton and Walsh. Other witnesses recalled the rise of Wheatley's fortunes in the locality: 'I mind the time when Johnnie Wheatley didna' hae as much as he's got the day and when he was in a grocer's shop and didna' chase the flies off his ham', one declared; and the allegation (without any foundation but dating from a journalists' strike at the *Eastern Standard* office the year before) surfaced once more that non-union labour was employed by Hoxton and Walsh. Wheatley seemed to lack confidence in his own appearances in the witness-box as the trial wore on, especially over the textual interpretation of speeches made several years earlier, and the question, hammered repeatedly by the defendants' counsel, of whether he had on public occasions ignored the National Anthem while he had been known in appropriate company to stand for the Irish 'Soldier's Song'.

Wheatley's son John recalled the strain the trial caused his father as it dragged on and the blow to him of the jury's verdict which went against him on both the actions he had brought before the court. After the verdict he recalled his father being visited by a member of the jury who had travelled to Glasgow to make known to him her misgivings over the behaviour of the jury foreman. He laid much stress, she insisted, on the presence of George V and Queen Mary in Edinburgh on a royal visit and told the jury never to forget that, whatever the merits of Wheatley's case, he was still a Socialist and a Roman Catholic.

Distress at the verdict and its visible effect upon Wheatley was widely felt within the labour movement, especially among those opposed to the influence of the drink trade. Emrys Hughes, commenting on the verdict for *Forward*, tried to put matters into perspective:

> Wheatley has no shares in the liquor trade but some of the shareholders who are in a minority and do not control his business,

happen to have. That is good enough for the Tory party into whose funds the brewers pour money like water.

The liquor trade is a powerful and insidious influence in our political life from which the Labour movement must keep itself free at all costs. From that point of view one wishes that Wheatley had even gone the length of refusing to have as his shareholders men who had made money out of the drink traffic.[23]

Such a refusal of any contamination by 'the trade' as Hughes admitted, would have been difficult for Wheatley or anybody to apply totally, given the extent of the brewers' influence and the major Scottish banks in which they were directors and shareholders. 'What really matters', Hughes concluded, 'to the electors of Shettleston, is that Wheatley, far from being in the pay of the drink traffic, has never been on the side of the trade politically, and actually voted for Prohibition in the House of Commons. That is his deadly sin.'[24] Hughes' article struck a different note from much of the Scottish press which took ill-concealed pleasure in Wheatley's defeat. Writing of the Tory campaign which had prompted the case and of Tory reaction to its result, Hughes hit upon the reality of the whole episode:

The deadly crime that this Catholic Irishman has committed is not the fact that he has been successful in his publishing business, but the fact that he still remembers his ten years in the Lanarkshire mines and is a leader in the party of the working class. They hate John Wheatley bitterly enough, but they hate the working-class and the Socialist movement more. To John Wheatley the businessman they have no objection but the Wheatley who uses his wealth and energies agitating for Socialism must be driven out of public life.[25]

Reid Miller's victory over Wheatley did not further his own political ambitions to the extent that he must have hoped. In fact, in 1928 the Shettleston Unionist Association dropped him in favour of another candidate to contest the seat. A drink problem may have been one factor in this but he embarked upon a bitter and divisive effort to win back the nomination, allying himself even more openly with Orange Lodges in the locality and making increasingly savage attacks on the Irish presence in Scotland. This was an activity in which he was kept company by some very public political figures who could write of Scotland's Irish community as breeding

> not merely unchecked but encouraged by their own medicine men. . . . They are responsible for most of the crime committed in Scotland, which otherwise would be the most law-abiding country in the world. Wheresoever knives and razors are used, wheresoever sneak-thefts and mean pilfering are easy and safe, wheresoever dirty acts of sexual baseness are committed there you will find the Irishman in Scotland with all but a monopoly of the business.[26]

The outcome of his court action did, indeed, take Wheatley close to resignation from Parliament, and MacDonald's advice may have been one factor which dissuaded him from this course of action. In a letter to Wheatley MacDonald put the issue in both personal and political terms:

> If you resign your seat now, that completes the victory for your enemies; if you propose to do it temporarily, you may find it difficult to get back, or at any rate to get a good opening. Then the interests of the movement ought to be studied. Would a by-election in Shettleston be a good thing at the present? Both Tories and Liberals could certainly confuse the issues and it looks as though the dice would be pretty badly loaded against us.[27]

Wheatley took his party leader's advice and rejected other advice that he might succeed in an appeal against the verdict on his case. For a time he retreated to the sanctuary of his home and family. By 1927 his children were grown up and at university; his daughter, Elizabeth, read medicine and his son, John, later joined the family business. His wife, Mary, had never sought a public role for herself, sharing platforms or electioneering with her husband, though she was always a party member and attended the more important meetings in her husband's constituency. After the move to Braehead House much of her time seems to have been spent looking after a family home bigger than any railway ganger's daughter could have ever imagined being responsible for, though she had the robust help about the house of a Mrs Ballantyne, who was long remembered in Shettleston for her association with the family.

Wheatley had a close relationship, too, with his brother, Patrick, and his family. Patrick Wheatley was actively involved in local politics and often entertained visiting speakers. His household is remembered as a hospitable place, though one in which no alcohol was ever in evidence, something it had in common with John Wheatley's home and, indeed, many Scottish Labour families at that time. Coming from such a large family, Wheatley felt it a duty to take an active interest in their well-being, something that one of them who is still alive, his niece Mrs Rose Viola, remembers with much warmth and gratitude. Education, both for his own family and for the local community, was high among his priorities, and while in Parliament he threw his weight behind moves to open a special school for the handicapped, Drumpark, which still exists.

Settling for his home and locality as a substitute for, and a refuge from, national politics was always an option for Wheatley, perhaps a tempting one after the strain of the 1927 court case. Speculation continued about his imminent retirement from Parliament and on 30 September of that year Dollan was quoted by the *New Leader* on the likelihood of Wheatley, in fact, resigning his seat. The steadfast support of his constituency's four ILP branches may have influenced him against this, however, and at the ILP's October Conference there were constant calls upon him not to resign. By then, anyway, he was back on the circuit of party meetings and addresses. A friendly press report of a Liverpool meeting he addressed along with Kirkwood and Dollan, described him as being back 'in great form'.[28]

III

During the period of Wheatley's preoccupation with defending his reputation locally, the ILP's problems in broadcasting and popularising its own policy statements had not diminished. They were worsened by the publication in June 1928 of the Cook–Maxton Manifesto. This was in part a response to the 'peace in industry' talks earlier in the year in which the TUC had agreed to take part with industrialists led by Sir Alfred Mond, Chairman of ICI. Ben Turner led the TUC in these talks, which were at once denounced by A. J. Cook, with all the fire and eloquence that had created his legendary reputation in the coalfields as a contemptible exercise in class collaboration.

The Cook–Maxton Manifesto proclaimed unswerving hostility to the assumption of any compatibility between socialism and capitalism, and reiterated the belief in 'an increasing war against poverty and working-class servitude' and that 'only by their own efforts can the workers obtain the fullest product of their labour'. Action was called for to mobilise rank and file opinion around the country behind the manifesto. 'Conditions have not changed', the manifesto finished by declaring, 'Wealth and property still flaunt themselves in the face of poverty-stricken workers who produce them. We ask you to join in the fight against the system which makes these conditions possible.'

Although Maxton and Cook put their names to this document, there has always been confusion over its actual authorship and over the relationship to it of Wheatley, who was quickly drawn into the bitter controversy it caused. At one level it can be seen as a bid by Maxton, the ILP's Chairman, to retrieve its radical credentials at a time when it was under constant communist attack for its reformism, and to use the manifesto against a Labour leadership with which he was openly at odds. He was at pains to deny any intention to bring about a Labour split: 'I am only going, if I can, to keep the party on the road where Keir Hardie set its feet.'[29]

John Paton and Fenner Brockway, however, have suggested that, although not a signatory, Wheatley was involved from the start. 'My impression', Brockway wrote later, 'is that in Wheatley's mind the campaign was a try-out. If it had concrete results, I believe he might have come out for a new political organization of the working class, incorporating the ILP but taking in other elements as well.'[30] His view that Wheatley was the moving spirit behind the manifesto was later endorsed by Willie Gallacher, who recalled taking Cook to the House of Commons for a meeting with Maxton which Wheatley attended along with Kirkwood, Buchannan and Stephen.[31] Gallacher's account was emphatic on Wheatley's support for the manifesto, but also on the importance he attached to avoiding a Labour split. Gallacher claimed he was assigned the task of writing the manifesto, though the British Communist Party's Central Committee later criticised it as weak and sentimental. Other accounts disagree over the actual authorship, but most attribute a central role to Wheatley, one of whose responsibilities was to have been the raising of finance for a campaign based upon the manifesto. Paton remains the strongest protagonist of the view that Wheatley was, by 1928, thinking in terms of a break with Labour: 'While Maxton was probably completely unaware of it, he had made the first move for the new party that Wheatley's ruthless mind conceived to be necessary.'[32]

There is insufficient evidence to substantiate this belief about Wheatley's motives, and he seems to have quickly lost whatever hopes he may have had about the manifesto's prospects for injecting new life into the movement. The way Maxton made the manifesto public, without consulting the ILP's National Administrative Council (NAC) or any of its divisional councils despite the fact that he was Party Chairman, alienated support from the very outset. Others close to Maxton, like Brockway and Paton, were not consulted in advance. The NAC endorsed his action only by a close vote, and strong opposition was voiced by Dollan at the ILP's July 1928 Scottish Conference. It avoided outright condemnation of Maxton but refused any official ILP backing for a manifesto campaign in Scotland. Wheatley continued to support Maxton in public but began to distance himself from the idea of a propaganda offensive to convert the rank and file.

The manifesto campaign got off to a bad start with a packed meeting in Glasgow's St Andrew's Hall at which Cook and Maxton gave unusually poor speeches. Wheatley was observed on the platform beside them carefully tearing up a cheque he had written out to give to the campaign funds, and, according to Gallacher, was furious after the speeches were over, pacing up and down muttering to himself. He recovered enough from his anger to arrange for adverts to go out promptly to the *Eastern Standard* and all the other Glasgow papers, publicising another meeting in Shettleston at which he would try to re-launch the manifesto. This and other meetings were held, but the manifesto's aspirations seemed to require at the very least a decisive Labour electoral victory. To Wheatley it was soon apparent that the way in which Cook and Maxton had played their hand would not contribute to such a victory. Gallacher was right in sensing that the campaign would fail, and it certainly both widened divisions between Labour and the ILP and

177

those within the ILP itself because of the way Maxton had endorsed the manifesto. After its failure there was little that either he or Wheatley could agree on with Dollan, yet neither of them could neutralise his power base within the Scottish ILP.

For Wheatley time was beginning to run out for further campaigns of the momentum that would have been needed to retrieve the fiasco of the manifesto's launching. Suffering increasingly from blood pressure and weight problems, he could no longer count on his own stamina to see him through, although he did intervene in the 1928 Labour Conference with a defence of Maxton, and castigated the policy document which was the nucleus of 'Labour and the Nation', the election programme for the next year, as 'the line of least resistance'.[33] He was angered by interruptions which he claimed came from the platform behind him, and Lansbury, in the chair, had to ask him to withdraw remarks he made about the 'calculated venom' being directed against him.[34]

Rumours persisted of Wheatley's impending break with Labour after the conference and he felt obliged to go into print to deny them, stressing instead the positive aspects of the situation within the party. 'The cold, machine-made card vote', he insisted, 'gave no indication at all of the throbbing enthusiasm for Socialism evident at the conference.'[35] Other articles he wrote at this time, however, reveal a deepening despair at what unemployment was doing to Glasgow and to his own constituency. Visits to the Parkhead Labour Exchange became something he dreaded, as men he had known for years tried to avoid being seen by their MP, such was the stigma that being without work carried for them. 'What foreign foe', Wheatley wrote during January 1929, 'could crush my friends into lower depths of humiliation than the British capitalist system has done.'[36] Angry demonstrations in Shettleston were common over rates of pay offered by the Parish Councils for relief work provided for the local unemployed. These, Wheatley's paper reported 'have elicited much sympathy locally owing to the obvious ravages of poverty in the physique and appearance of the men. The processions are noteworthy for the big number of men affected on whose breasts glitter the medals they received at the conclusion of military service in the Great War.'[37] Niggardly though parish Councils could be in their treatment of the long-term unemployed, Labour could still put up candidates at elections to them, and Wheatley joined in Labour's attack in the Commons on legislation by the Baldwin government which would abolish them. The real reason, he was clear in his own mind, was to prevent any recurrence of the 'Poplarism' of the early 1920s.

By this time a general election was imminent, for few believed Baldwin would wish his government to serve out the full five years to which it was, in law, entitled. Parliament was, in fact, dissolved on 18 May, 1929, and Baldwin conducted a low-key campaign despite the greatly enlarged electorate created by the Representation of the People Act the previous year. In Shettleston, talk of Wheatley's retirement was soon forgotten in an enthusiastic campaign, in which the twenty-four year old Jennie Lee, a candidate herself in North Lanark, arrived to support his campaign. The Shettleston Labour Party issued a leaflet on Wheatley's behalf, entitled 'Hard Facts', and the *Eastern Standard* gave its entire front page to his presentation of Labour policy. All the themes he had pursued in opposition since 1924 were condensed into a rational and ethical statement of the socialist case. He finished by declaring:

> Socialism alone can save Britain. It can make her again the leader in civilization. . . Let us unite then to end the dark days of scarcity, unemployment, ignorance, disease, hatred, strife, war,

179

oppression and national antagonisms, and confident in ourselves, our mission and our ideal, raise ourselves and our nation to a higher and more glorious plane.[38]

Wheatley's majority, in sharp contrast to the close result in 1924, was 6,724; all the Clydesiders were returned with secure majorities. Labour itself won 287 seats, becoming for the first time the biggest single party in Parliament, though still in a minority there and in the country at large. Baldwin, ignoring those who urged a Conservative–Liberal coalition to keep Labour out, advised the King to send for MacDonald rather than involve himself in any overtures to Lloyd George, whom he deeply distrusted.

There was, it seems, a division of opinion within the Labour leadership as to whether Wheatley should be invited to join the government. Snowden and Henderson led those who favoured the lesser evil, as they saw it, of bringing him in, but as Snowden later recalled, 'MacDonald was strongly opposed to offering him a post in the new government. Wheatley had deserted and insulted us, and MacDonald thought the country would be shocked if he were included in the Cabinet, and it would be taken as evidence of rebel influence.'[39] Wheatley, of course, had already committed himself publicly against serving in another minority Labour government and put his case to a full meeting of the parliamentary Labour Party after the election. His voice was virtually a lone one this time, for most of the ILP group accepted the view of the newly elected Brockway that the government should be supported on condition that it developed a socialist programme on pensions and unemployment which could be taken to the country in another election if a Conservative–Liberal alliance voted it down. Wheatley made one of his most powerful speeches, cautioning the leadership against falling into the trap of trying to administer a capitalist system in deepening crisis in which the working class would be prime victims. Better far, he urged, to throw the responsibility on parties who professed to believe in the system. 'There was', Brockway remembered, 'a quality of strength and certainty in his voice, and his reasoning was masterly and remorseless. Two minutes after he had risen on this occasion, the members forgot their impatience with criticism at the moment of triumph: they listened and temporarily they were convinced, despite themselves.'[40] But it was temporarily, for the die was cast and Labour was embarked upon a second and disastrous lesson on the difference between merely holding office and exercising power.

IV

Divisions between the government and the ILP, and divisions within the ILP, were apparent almost from the moment the new Parliament opened. Wheatley, Maxton, Kirkwood and others tabled an amendment to the King's speech which was both radical and comprehensive in its terms. It demanded for every worker 'an income, including children's allowances, sufficient to meet the human needs of himself and his family, and measures aimed at the re-organization of the industrial system so that it shall provide for the needs of the community, by nationalizing the key sources of industrial power'.[41]

Not only was the parliamentary leadership angered but Dollan and Shinwell claimed that the ILP group of members had not been properly consulted. Such consultation would, of course, have stifled the amendment right away, for most ILP MPs were in all respects identical in their views to the party leadership and held no brief for the views of Maxton and Wheatley. This reality posed inescapable questions about the continuing relationship of the ILP to the Parliamentary Party and, indeed, the movement as a whole. By 1929 Wheatley and

Maxton were activists in a parliamentary faction that could have been out-voted on all the major initiatives it attempted had all the 105 members who had ILP membership cards chosen to attend its group meetings at Westminster.

It was the active core of the ILP which took up the challenge of exposing the shortcomings of Labour government policy. Their chosen targets were Margaret Bondfield, whose task it was to steer through Parliament a National Insurance Bill; and J. H. (Jimmy) Thomas, whose ministerial brief included preparing unspecified measures to tackle mounting unemployment. The fight against the 'not genuinely seeking work' clauses of the Bondfield bill, which would add substantially to the discretion of officials in setting levels of benefit, was a bitter one. So, too, was the attack directed by Wheatley and Maxton upon actual payments under the bill, which were only two-thirds of what Labour's own representatives had called for in their evidence to the Blanesborough Committee on Unemployment, which had reported in 1927.

This guerrilla campaign against the government on the floor of the Commons and in the division lobbies was a constant drain on its energies and brought from Wheatley what turned out to be a final show of the cold steel which had earned him his reputation in debate virtually from the moment of his election to Parliament. J. H. Thomas, chairman of a cabinet committee comprising Mosley, Johnston and Lansbury to co-ordinate schemes for the creation of employment, was perhaps his most hapless victim. Brockway recalled one relentless sequence of questions by Wheatley concerning the measurable benefits to the unemployed of Thomas's work:

> After some hesitation Thomas admitted that the work provided was insignificant compared with the money spent. By now it was clear that Wheatley was bursting Thomas's balloon. He rose a third time and in his dry, matter of fact way gave the final piercing

stab. There was nothing for Thomas to do but gather the deflated wreckage.[42]

Wheatley perhaps knew a soft target when he saw one and seemed to lose his relish for the pursuit of Thomas. It is not clear either whether at this stage he saw himself as the arbiter of the government's fate, though this was how some commentators were beginning to describe him:

> The Clydeside leader is not a popular figure, but he commands the support of one who is, Mr Maxton, and the loyalty of a group which holds the key to the present parliamentary situation. It is no exaggeration to say that the fate of the government depends more upon Mr Wheatley than upon Mr Lloyd George. When the final crisis comes, his will be the hand that will strike Mr MacDonald and his colleagues from power. It is not a hand that will flinch from the task.[43]

The final crisis for the government, though Wheatley would not live to see it, took a form which denied any decisive role to the ILP. In his final months there were those who saw him as a calculating but inscrutable figure, but his performance at the January 1930 Scottish ILP Divisional Conference belied that impression. The ILP's National Council had already delivered a statement congratulating those Labour MPs who had opposed the government's Unemployment Insurance Bill, and the Scottish conference had to debate a resolution endorsing this. Dollan vacated the chair to support an amendment to the resolution, so concerned was he not to lose his hold over the party in Scotland. This tactic succeeded and the attempt to identify the conference with Maxton, Wheatley and the other Labour rebels was defeated; 103 delegates voted for the amendment and ninety-four for the original resolution.

Wheatley went to the rostrum in fighting form, and poured scorn upon the Treasury brief from which ministers had defended a real breach of faith with the unemployed: 'No one had asked the Government for anything it was impossible to obtain. They were told the money was not there, but would the Chancellor of the Exchequer, in the event of an invasion of this country, say that the till was empty and that the invasion would have to be postponed?'[44] The *New Leader* thought the speech one of the best Wheatley had ever given to a Labour gathering, and described how it closed 'with a sustained and moving piece of eloquence in which he asked the delegates to uphold the leadership of James Maxton in his native land. Was Maxton only to speak for England, was he to be disowned at home?'[45]

Outside Scotland, the major ILP divisional councils stood by Maxton at their conference, and it was clear that a breaking point could not be far off in the relationship of ILP members who shared the views of Maxton and Wheatley and the Parliamentary Labour party as a whole. Those close to Wheatley were left unsure whether he would endorse a final break, notwithstanding the closeness of his relationship to Maxton. His doubts turned at times into depression, affected also by visibly declining health.

A vivid impression of Wheatley just over a couple of months before his death was recorded by Beatrice Webb, who six years before had seen him as the coming man of Labour's front bench in Parliament. Her opinion of the Clydesiders had never been particularly high, but in her judgement, as in that of others, Wheatley' ability had always stood out. This, no doubt, was why she felt obliged to stress the decline that she felt was apparent in him by February 1930: 'John Wheatley came to my Wednesday lunch. He has deteriorated mentally and physically since I knew him as a member of MacDonald's 1924 Cabinet. As a Cabinet Minister he was a brilliant success – alike in his department and in the House. As a rebel in the

party he has been a failure.'[46] Her diary entry enlarged upon
Wheatley's appearance and general demeanour: 'His expression
is sullen, his words are bitter; his lips are blue and his com-
plexion is patchy – and he closes his eyes at you.'[47] These
visible signs of illness made less impression on her, however,
than the conversation she recalled: 'He says that he has lost his
faith in political democracy: the common people have no will
of their own, they are swayed backwards and forwards. He
would be a Communist if he were not a pious Catholic. As it
is, he has no consistent position, and will, I imagine, drop out
of politics.'[48]

What Mrs Webb knew, or imagined she knew, of
Wheatley's background influenced her judgement that he could
have made a successful career in some other political system:
'In the USA he would have succeeded as a local boss. He is a
good mob orator and would have revelled in the intrigue and
corruption of the machine; he would have been acute and
good-natured in dispensing offices and bribes among his followers. But he lacks the sanity and honourableness needed for success in British politics.'[49] Whether either or both of these
virtues were in superbundant supply in British politics in the
inter-war years remains debatable, and her judgements upon
Wheatley in this entry were not so different from those of his
Tory-Orange detractors in Glasgow whom he had sued in
1927. Possibly, the low spirits in which Wheatley appears in
the diary were a product of the notoriously spartan fare on
offer when the Webbs entertained, for he always enjoyed a
good lunch. He does seem to have rallied later on in this
meeting with a caustic and wide-ranging critique of the Labour
movement and its leaders, and the entry goes on to mention
that Wheatley was much amused by the suggestion of his host-
ess that his real role might be as the Vatican's first ambassador
to Moscow.

Despite a widely observed deterioration in his health, Wheatley managed to remain active in a variety of ways in the remainder of February and March. Late in March he made a point of attending Parliament to vote for an ILP member's resolution calling upon the government to prepare the ground for general disarmament by an annual reduction in its own arms bill, also by ending all state grants-in-aid of officer training at schools and universities. Apart from Wheatley and Maxton, just twenty-one other members went into the division lobby on this motion. The week-end after this found him in Sheffield attending a series of Labour meetings and holding his own with hecklers during an address he had been asked to give on the theme of socialism and unemployment.

Wheatley's health began to give real cause for concern at the ILP's April 1930 Conference in Birmingham. This was a gathering of great importance in so far as it served to define sharply the issues between the ILP and the Labour Party, especially where ILP voting rights in Parliament were concerned, and to reiterate the liberty of action which the ILP reserved for itself on issues of socialist principle. Wheatley, against medical advice, had travelled to Birmingham for the conference and collapsed during it, and was still recovering in his hotel when the vital debate on the ILP's role in Parliament took place.

Brockway visited Wheatley in his hotel during the conference and was shocked at his physical deterioration. In fact, he had only a short time still to live but summoned up the strength for some final activity. His last newspaper article read like a retrospect on a political lifetime and a justification of his own stance within the labour movement. This was written for the *Daily Herald* on 28 April 1930 and all his old polemical vigour was displayed for one last time. It was entitled 'Why I am a Rebel', and much of it was taken up with his childhood and early life, and the forces that had shaped his political development. He described himself as one of Keir Hardie's converts to socialism and used Hardie's rectitude as a standard from which to flay the shortcomings of the Labour leadership: 'Can you see Hardie strutting and posing in cloth of blue and gold ? Can you see him flunkeying in knee breeches, tripping and fumbling with his sword? Can you imagine Hardie with £5,000 a year preaching thrift to you workers with 30 shillings or £2 a week?'[50] Hardie had been, above all, a courageous rebel against brutal injustice, and now Wheatley stressed that, given capitalism's hugely increased potential for production, the gulf between rich and poor was, in fact, greater than in his child-hood. In principle then, he argued, the movement's task had not changed, though pressure upon its leaders to keep faith with that task was more urgent than ever. He concluded:

> Make no mistake about this. No rebel has yet cast a vote in Parliament except for something which was the declared policy of the Party. We are not in rebellion against the Labour Party, but we are in rebellion against anybody who will try to lead it away from its great historic mission. That mission was the abolition of poverty. Until that task is accomplished every Labour man and woman ought to be a rebel.'[51]

Just over two weeks later Wheatley became ill again after putting in a full week's work in Parliament, believing he had recovered from his collapse during the ILP's Birmingham Conference. His doctors had advised him against returning to Parliament so soon, and his decision to travel back to Glasgow on Friday 12 May may have been fatal. He died late that night from a brain haemorrhage shortly after arriving at his home in Shettleston.

Obituaries and tributes came in profusion, many of them in papers that he had often contributed to himself. All agreed on the gap that his passing would create and on the talents he had brought to the political stage during his short period under the spotlight of national politics. The *New Statesman* reflected:

> As long as he lived he was always a big potential force, possibly the one man who had the power of making his former colleagues feel uncomfortable. The ILP rump is likely to be very much weakened by his death and possibly the Labour Party itself may be weakened too, for the quarrel might have been mended, and Mr Wheatley might have come back to the influence which his ability seemed to fit him to enjoy.[52]

His burial on 15 May 1930 was the biggest political funeral Glasgow had seen since the death of John MacLean six years before. His wife and family had hoped that it might be kept a private occasion, but nothing could prevent the crowds lining the grey streets of Shettleston in the rain to pay their last respects to a man who had served them well as councillor, Member of Parliament and minister. Prominent among the mourners was Oswald Mosley, soon to resign from the Labour government in order to travel a road along which Wheatley would never have kept political company with him. Mosley's wreath of red roses, Wheatley's niece later recalled, was the largest floral tribute on his coffin. Along with Mosley, Neville Chamberlain and many Labour MPs walked a haggard and grief-stricken James Maxton to whom Brockway had had to break the news after both had attended a series of socialist meetings in Holland and Belgium.

John Wheatley was laid to rest in Dalbeth cemetery on Glasgow's London Road, where many of the very poorest of the city's immigrant Irish had been buried over two genera-tions. To the end of his life, Wheatley never forgot that he had been one of them. Crowds packed the cemetery as they had lined the route to it. 'Workmen', John Scanlon later wrote, 'dropped their hammers and picks to go and pay their last respects to one of their own.'[53] More than all the numerous obituaries and appreciations in the local and national press, this last tribute by Wheatley's people would have mattered to him most.

He left over £16,000 to his family, a substantial house, which still stands, and a controlling interest in Hoxton and Walsh, which he had turned into a prosperous business. Both his children were at university when he died, his son John studying medicine in Dublin and his daughter Elizabeth following the same course in Glasgow. Ultimately the son joined the family business, while Elizabeth settled in England after qualifying, working first in Burnley and later in London as a school medical adviser. Neither, however, achieved the prominence of his brother Patrick's son. He was called to the Scottish bar, reintroduced the family name to Parliament as Labour MP for East Edinburgh from 1947 to 1954, and became Lord Advocate and eventually Lord Justice Clerk of Scotland.

9 Conclusions

Tom Gallagher has written perceptively of how Scotland came to terms with its Irish immigrant community without sectarianism ever assuming an ascendant political role.[1] Outward mobility from the confines of a close-knit expatriate culture contributed to this, and John Wheatley's talents enabled him to become a conspicuous example of the process. With or without some resolution of the Irish Question after the First World War, United Irish League politics in Baillieston and Shettleston would have become a cul-de-sac for him. At least until 1914, however, he retained his contacts with the League, partly through his role in the Catholic Socialist Society, but his Catholicism remained the most important part of his Irish identity. This is clear from his support for the 1918 Education (Scotland) Act and his choice of fee-paying Catholic schools for his children.

Politically, his life embodies the convergence of Irish immigrant nationalism in Scotland with an indigenous working class beginning to feel its way towards support for a labour movement that would dare to seek independence from existing parties and develop a socialist programme of its own. Wheatley's attempts to synthesise his Catholicism with his socialism involved him in serious clashes with individual clergy, but such conflict did not offer a serious impediment to the process of convergence. There were political opponents who attacked him politically for his Catholicism, but they had a hard task to characterise him as being in politics simply as the church's man.

This, with the exception of the question of birth control in 1924, he never was, either as councillor or MP, and it was not a role in which he was seen by the Moderator of the General Assembly of the Church of Scotland, who was among the mourners at his funeral in 1930.

His political career was made in a labour movement conscious of its Scottish identity and committed to Scottish Home Rule from the moment of its foundation. For Wheatley, with his early years given over to Irish nationalist politics, there could have been no denying the justice of that cause, but once in Parliament, he came increasingly to approach the issues of the moment and the broader goal of achieving socialism within the framework of an Anglo-British state.

There is reason to regret this, for recent events have shown just how vulnerable local democracy is to the inroads of a state machine controlled by the radical right. As Health Minister in 1924, Wheatley, in his defence of Poplar and in his Housing Act, achieved much for elected local government, but he tended from then until his death to argue in terms of control of the state as an end in itself for socialists. Yet as a communicator and debater he could have done much to sustain debate on how best to recast that state into an instrument of democratic socialist change. In such a debate the issue of Scottish self-government could have been kept central to Labour's priorities, but in his final years Wheatley had little to contribute to this. His last general election campaign in 1929 was devoid of references to Scotland's constitutional relationship to England, and in a special election article he described the contest as one between the parties of 'nation-breakers' and 'nation-builders'. The nation he was concerned with, however, was a British nation: 'Socialism alone can save Britain', he declared, 'It can make her again the leader in civilization.'[2] Labour was on the way to becoming a unionist party and, as such, a target for criticism by those who wished to emphasise the specifically Scottish dimension of politics.

The frustrations of contemporary Scottish Labour, confronting and often winning the political argument against a Thatcher government with no Scottish mandate, have served to re-open debate on the nature of the British state and whether socialist advance within its archaic structure is still possible. Tom Nairn and Neal Ascherson have eloquently made the case for it being taken apart and rebuilt in a way which would create real citizenship and recognise the cultural pluralism of these islands. The cultivated irreverence of Wheatley and the other Clydeside MPs for Westminster convention was no substitute for hard analysis of the nature of state power itself. There was, of course, in the last years of his life, one working model of devolved power at Stormont in Belfast, but it was hardly one with which Wheatley, given his background, could identify. He was a victim, too, of his success as a minister in 1924, which contributed to a shrinking of his vision of alternative constitutional forms which socialists could use. He did at least, in 1927, join Tom Johnston in support of the Rev. James Barr's bill not just to devolve power but to achieve dominion status for Scotland. The bill had no chance of success and was talked out, and by then Wheatley had little more to say on constitutional or national questions.

Given what became the narrowing confines of his conception of socialist advance within the existing British state, Wheatley had a shrewd sense of procedural strategy, whether in Glasgow City Chambers or at Westminster. He was never mesmerised by such issues, however, and was ready to take part in acts of defiance of parliamentary rules if he thought political advantage for Labour would be the result. Nor did he lose sight of the pressure which mass action, perhaps in contravention of unjust laws enacted without mandate, could apply from outside to

Parliament or the Council Chamber. Without this conviction he could not have given the support that he did to the Glasgow rent strikes of 1915 and 1920, nor to the General Strike in 1926. Reformist he may be, to those who see Scottish labour history simply as a catalogue of class betrayals, but he did not disdain the word in so far as reform meant tackling tuberculosis or getting houses built for working-class families.

His 1924 Housing Act remains the achievement for which he is best remembered, though he was always aware of its limitations, as he was of his failure to push through Parliament the essential related legislation on the control of building materials. His handling of this legislation brought him to the centre of the political stage and convinced observers like Beatrice Webb, Oswald Mosley, Charles Masterman and Ramsay MacDonald that he was one of Labour's coming men.

The frustrations of office in a minority Labour government proved to be greater for Wheatley than the rewards, and Labour's defeat in 1924 freed him to join with Maxton and others in developing a radical critique of the threadbare formulations of MacDonald and Snowden. Did Wheatley make an effective contribution to this, and had he a secure base within the broad labour movement from which to develop it and mobilise support? These questions must be addressed if any evaluation of his place in labour history is to be possible.

Labour's dilemma after 1918 was, in essence, to pursue apparently radical goals with little more than the tools of orthodox Gladstonian financial policy. Wheatley was able to see this, and though not an intellectual innovator himself, assimilated from Hobson and Brailsford alternative strategies which kept alive the movement's aspirations to social justice while offering it the means, in office, to lift the economy out of recession. 'Socialism in Our Time' and the 'Living Wage' document upon which it was based have been represented as attempts simply to rationalise capitalism, and there is truth in the charge if it implies that those who supported it saw economic growth as the surest base from which to fund family allowances and a minimum wage through redistributive taxation, and gave priority to this over immediate programmes of public ownership. A more basic problem remains the ambiguous character of this programme and whether it could produce a recognisably socialist outcome or merely a reformed capitalist system.

Wheatley certainly saw this as a chance to mobilise the movement behind a programme which offered an answer to mass poverty and mass unemployment, but rejected both Free Trade and simple protectionism in favour of planning and controls over trade with other countries. Above all, though, he responded to this strategy because it treated unemployment as the result of lack of consumer demand in the economy, for which only the minimum wage strategy could provide a remedy by raising basic working-class spending power. His enthusiasm was more genuine than for the much more militant Cook–Maxton Manifesto, though he gave the latter his public support. While the manifesto was widely represented as a divisive polemic, at least the 'Living Wage' doctrine was remitted by the 1926 Labour Party Conference to a Committee of Inquiry. This response was perhaps added reason for Wheatley's disappointment when so little of it was incorporated within 'Labour and the Nation' or in the 1929 election programme.

The 'Socialism in Our Time' document and the Labour Party Commission which deliberated on it after the 1926 Conference might not have paid enough attention to the need for private and public investment in industry and might have neglected the relationship between monetary policy and cur-rency movements, but it offered more than its detractors would allow at the time. This is certainly the verdict of recent work on the period by Gordon Brown, William Knox and F. M. Leventhal, all of whom argue that Wheatley was right to identify and support attainable policy goals which emerged from these debates. The post-1945 Labour government did, after all, carry out some of them in its commitment to welfare and full employment.

Where major policy initiatives like these were concerned, Wheatley's problem was that his talents as a debater and communicator could not compensate for the lack of a secure power base within the movement. He was right to identify himself with a Labour left that had a clear policy alternative to the leadership rather than concentrating its efforts on issues relating to mechanisms of accountability within the party that meant little to the electorate, perhaps the central failure of Tony Benn and his supporters in the late 1970s and early 1980s. The ILP, however, had existed on borrowed time since 1918, refusing either to submerge itself within the Labour Party or to retreat into a purely propagandist role. What held it together until 1925 was Clifford Allen's tireless work as the Chairman and the funds he was able to tap in order to overhaul its structure and appoint more full-time officials.

Even so, it had passed its membership peak by the time that Wheatley's alienation from the Labour leadership was a reality, and even in Scotland the support he could expect from it was uncertain, as the Scottish Divisional Council's backing for the Dollan–Johnston line against him over the Cook–Maxton Manifesto made very clear. In his own Shettleston constituency matters were different, for there the ILP virtually was the Labour Party and he had a local status that was virtually independent of the case he argued against MacDonald and Snowden. He often did this in his own pages of the *Glasgow Eastern Standard*, which, however, succeeded more as a community newspaper than it ever did as a vehicle for his views on policy debates within the labour movement as a whole.

Where, then, could Wheatley have looked in order to mobilise support for the policy alternatives he supported? Not to the Communist Party, though he kept in touch with Gallacher and in the degree of support he gave the Cook–Maxton Manifesto he was not deterred by that party's role in bringing the signatories together. On the other hand, he had never committed himself as far as Maxton to support for communist affiliation to Labour, though, by 1928, Labour conference majorities against it, as well as Moscow's emerging line of open war on non-communist parties, had virtually killed the idea. The communists, for their part, had given priority to industrial struggle and to the creation of their own organisation within the unions in the form of the National Minority Movement. The basic political split within the unions was still over the communist/anti-communist conflict, and this left little scope for a distinctively ILP presence in most unions.

Wheatley, in fact, had no base within the unions, and Cook was the only major union leader with whom, through Maxton, he established any sort of relationship. The unions in any case were divided within their own ranks over their response to the National Minority Movement, crippled by the defeat of the General Strike and the punitive legislation which followed it, then further divided over 'Mondism', the TUC General Council's favourable response to invitations from Sir Alfred Mond of ICI and other employers to discuss areas of common interest. None of this left much scope for Wheatley or Maxton to make much of a case within the TUC or individual unions for an innovative policy document like 'Socialism in Our Time'. With its concern to stimulate demand, it would have needed a form of wage or income control to make it inflation-proof, something no union leaders would tolerate then or later. Wheatley's predicament was, thus, in the late 1920s, to be a challenger to Labour's leadership on grounds which no significant element within the unions would share with him.

Other left oppositions to Labour policy would face similar problems, like the Socialist League in the 1930s and the Bevanite left of the 1950s. The latter group did build up some significant support within some unions, but could never convert this into an effective challenge to the immobilism of right-wing union bureaucracies.

Wheatley, in the last year or two of his life, was also a leading figure in a left opposition, arguing against a lacklustre leadership, a case that was principled and intellectually coherent. His base from which to do this, the ILP, was a crumbling one, and when the second Labour government was formed in 1929 he had been driven back to a back-bench *franc-tireur*'s role in Parliament, though still making whatever use he could of the labour movement's press to make his voice heard. This, in his final days, was how he still reached many in the movement.

Wheatley's performance in his final months in Parliament, using every debate and many divisions to push with Maxton for the ILP's minimum demands, has tempted some writers to believe that he was, in fact, on course for the final severance with Labour which took place after his death. Some writers on Labour in the 1920s have accepted this. Paton and Scanlon were of the opinion that when he gave his backing to the Cook–Maxton Manifesto in 1928, he was preparing the ground for a new socialist grouping. Wheatley's speeches and articles at the time give no support for such a view, but the ILP's actual disaffiliation from Labour so soon after his death has led to conflicting claims as to which side he would have taken.

The principle of disaffiliation was, in fact, debated at the April 1930 ILP Conference which Wheatley attended but from which he had to absent himself because of rapidly deteriorating health. Resolutions were adopted at the conference ordering the National Council of the ILP to reconstruct the party's parliamentary group on the basis of acceptance of ILP policy as laid down by the party's annual conference and interpreted by the Council. No ILP candidates for Parliament, the resolutions made clear, were to be endorsed by the Council except on this basis. Middlemas argued that this was the penultimate step to disaffiliation and claimed, too, that Wheatley saw 'the irretrievable danger of the extremists' exclusion policy at Birmingham',[3] but he was too ill to leave his hotel room for the debate. Brockway visited Wheatley at this time and left him uncertain as to what his intentions would be if it came to an ILP break with Labour.

More recently, however, Brockway was of the opinion that Wheatley would have supported Maxton on the issue of changes in the Parliamentary Labour Party's Standing Orders acceptable to the ILP while seeking to avoid a final break.[4] Whether he could have sustained such a position must remain doubtful, but Brockway's view accords with that of many accounts of the disaffiliation crisis in which Wheatley's removal from the scene is treated as a critical factor. This does less than justice to Maxton's ability to make his own decision, and also neglects the extent of Wheatley's own disenchantment with Labour under MacDonald's leadership.

It is, of course, possible that Wheatley and Maxton would have taken opposed positions over disaffiliation, for much as Maxton admired Wheatley, he was never totally under his influence. Their political relationship had been complementary, as their different roles in the Cook–Maxton Manifesto campaign had shown, but it must remain questionable whether Wheatley, with all his conspicuous political talents and his concern for immediate and effective reforms, would have accepted for long the purity of impotence which was how Aneurin Bevan described the ILP's position after 1932. His doubts over which road the ILP should best travel underline for us the perennial problem of any independent socialist body which seeks a role distinct from that of the Labour party.

Notes

Chapter 1

Some of the material used in this chapter has already appeared in an article by me, 'John Wheatley, the Irish, and the labour movement in Scotland', in the *Innes Review*, 21, Autumn (1980). Valuable evidence on Wheatley's early life can be found in an unpublished autobiographical manuscript by Patrick Dollan, and in a series of articles he wrote, 'Memories of fifty years ago', for the *Mercat Cross* magazine in 1953. There is also useful material in Wheatley's own leaflets: *Mines, Miners and Misery*, (Glasgow, 1909) and *How the Miners are Robbed* (Glasgow, 1907). S. Jackson's *My Ain Folk* is a most useful history of Baillieston and district.

1 P. J. Dollan, 'Memories of fifty years ago', *Mercat Cross*, 6, 1953, p. 72.
2 W. Walker, 'Irish immigrants in Scotland: their priests, politics and parochial life', *Historical Journal*, 15 (1972), pp. 649–67.

Chapter 2

1 *Glasgow Observer*, 27 December 1900.
2 *Ibid.*, 27 July 1901.
3 Compton MacKenzie, *Catholicism and Scotland* (London, 1936), p. 185.
4 Shettleston ILP Minutes, 26 April 1908.
5 *Glasgow Observer*, 24 February 1906.
6 *Forward*, 6 July 1912.
7 *Glasgow Observer*, 3 November 1906.
8 *Ibid.*, 24 November 1906.
9 J. Wheatley, *The Catholic Working Man* (Glasgow, 1909).
10 *Glasgow Observer*, 30 March 1907.
11 *Ibid.*
12 *Ibid.*, 19 October 1907.
13 S. Gilley, 'Catholics and Socialists in Glasgow', in K. Lunn (ed.), *Hosts, Immigrants and Minorities: Historial Responses to Newcomers in British Society* (London, 1980), p. 188.
14 J. Wheatley, *Mines, Miners and Misery* (Glasgow, 1909).
15 *Ibid.*, p. 22.
16 *Ibid.*, p. 17.

17 *Ibid.*, p. 8.
18 *Forward*, 28 November 1909.
19 Quoted in Gilley, *op. cit.*, p. 189.
20 J. McGovern, *Neither Fear Nor Favour* (London, 1960), p. 40.
21 *Forward*, 29 July 1912.
22 One is a letter to me from John Wheatley's son, the late John Patrick Wheatley (in my possession).
23 J. Scanlon, *Book of the Labour Party*, edited by H. Tracey, III (London, 1925), p. 210.
24 *Forward*, 6 July 1912.

Chapter 3

1 *Glasgow Observer*, 7 November 1912.
2 *The Times*, 24 October 1902.
3 D. Englander, 'Landlord and tenant in urban Scotland: the background to the Clyde rent strikes, 1915', *Journal of Scottish Labour History Society* 15 (1981), pp. 4–14.
4 *Glasgow Evening Times*, 29 November 1912.
5 J. Wheatley's evidence to Royal Commission on Housing of the Industrial Population of Scotland, 1917–18, para. 22, 634.
6 J. Wheatley, *Eight Pound Cottages for Glasgow Citizens* (Glasgow, 1913), p. 5.
7 J. Wheatley, *A Christian in Difficulties* (Glasgow, 1912).
8 *Ibid.*
9 *Forward*, 14 March 1914.
10 W.Gallacher, *Revolt on the Clyde* (London, 1980, reprint), p. 22.
11 J. Scanlon in H. Tracey (ed.), *The Book of the Labour Party*, III (London, 1925), pp. 211–12.
12 H. McShane and J. Smith, *Harry McShane – No Mean Fighter* (London, 1978), p. 27.

Chapter 4

1 R. E. Dowse, *Left in the Centre* (London, 1966) p. 20.
2 D. Kirkwood, *My Life of Revolt* (London, 1935), p. 87.
3 *Forward*, 13 November 1915.
4 *Ibid.*, 13 March 1915.
5 *Ibid.*, 12 June 1915.
6 *Ibid.*, 19 June 1915.
7 *Ibid.*,
8 *Ibid.*, 30 October 1915.
9 Kirkwood, *op. cit.*, pp. 117 – 18.
10 *Ibid.*
11 A. Marwick, *The Deluge* (London, 1965), p. 76.

12 R.K. Middlemas, *The Clydesiders* (London, 1965), pp. 68–9. J. Hinton in *The First Shop Stewards Movement* (London, 1973), p. 150, argues that Middlemas is closer to the truth of Wheatley's role than are other accounts.

13 W. Gallacher, *Revolt on the Clyde* (London, 1980 reprint), p. 23.

14 *Glasgow Herald*, 13 April 1917.

15 *Forward*, 1 January 1917.

16 *Ibid.*, 8 December 1917.

17 *Forward*, 26 February 1916.

18 *Ibid.*, 26 January 1916.

19 *Ibid.*,

20 *Ibid.*, 9 February 1918.

Chapter 5

1 *Forward*, 7 December 1918.

2 *Glasgow Herald*, 11 December 1918.

3 *Glasgow Observer*, 26 October 1918.

4 *Forward*, 14 December 1918.

5 *Ibid.*

6 *Ibid.*, 24 January 1920.

7 Royal Commission on Housing of Industrial Population of Scotland (Urban and Rural) 1917–18.

8 J. Wheatley, T*he New Rent Act – A Reply to the Rent Raisers* (Glasgow 1920), p. 4.

9 *Forward*, 14 August 1920.

10 STUC Report, 1921, pp. 38–9.

11 *Glasgow Herald*, 9 September 1921, Bruce Murray News Cuttings Book.

12 *Ibid.*

13 J. Scanlon, *Decline and Fall of the Labour Party* (London, 1932), p. 29.

14 *Forward*, 25 November 1922.

15 *Ibid.*, 25 November 1922.

16 *Ibid.*

17 *Ibid.*

18 *Ibid.*

19 *The Times*.

20 E.Shinwell, *Conflict Without Malice* (London, 1955), p. 77.

21 J. Paton, *Left Turn* (London, 1936), p. 150.

Chapter 6

1 D. Kirkwood, *My Life of Revolt* (London, 1935), pp. 194–5.

2 Parliamentary Debates, 23 November 1922, vol. 159, paras 97–101.

3 *Ibid.*, 24 April 1923, vol. 163, para. 325.

4 *Ibid.*, para. 330.
5 *Ibid.*,para. 335.
6 *Ibid.*,
7 Ibid., 13 February 1923, vol. 160, paras 101–7.
8 *Ibid.*
9 *Ibid.*, 8 May 1923, vol. 163, para. 2,225.
10 *Ibid.*, 27 June 1923, vol. 165, para. 2,379.
11 *Ibid.*, para. 2,388.
12 *The Times*, 28 June 1923.
13 T. N. Graham, *Willie Graham* (London, 1948), p. 134.
14 *New Leader*, 29 June 1923.
15 *Ibid.*
16 *Glasgow Herald*, 9 July 1923.
17 A. F. Brockway, *Towards Tomorrow* (London, 1977), p. 66.
18 *Daily Dispatch*, 2 July 1923.
19 *New Leader*, 2 July 1923.
20 A. J. P. Taylor, *English History* (Oxford, 1965) p. 203.
21 *New Leader*, 2 March 1923.
22 *Ibid.*, 6 April 1923.
23 ILP Conference Report, 1923, pp. 88–91.
24 *Ibid.*
25 J. Wheatley, *Starving in the Midst of Plenty* (Glasgow, 1923), p. 5.
26 *Ibid.*
27 *Ibid.*
28 *New Leader*, 30 March 1923.
29 ILP Conference Report, 1923, p. 143.
30 R. E. Dowse, *Left in the Centre* (London, 1966) p. 93.
31 Kirkwood, *op. cit.*, p. 202.
32 *Forward*, 3 November 1923.
33 *Ibid.*
34 *Ibid.*, 15 December 1923.
35 *Ibid.*
36 *Ibid.*

Chapter 7

1 PRO 30/69, p. 668, MacDonald to Henderson, 22 December 1923.
2 D. Marquand, *Ramsay MacDonald* (London, 1977), p. 304.
3 P. Dollan, unpublished autobiography, p. 26.
4 H. Nicholson, *King George V* (London, 1952), p. 389.
5 K. Morgan and J. Morgan, *Portrait of a Progressive* (Oxford, 1980), p. 109.
6 M. A. Hamilton, *Fit to Govern* (London, 1924), pp. 33–4.
7 J. Scanlon, *Cast Off All Fooling* (London, 1938), pp. 152–3.

8 *The Times*, 9 February 1924.

9 P. Snowden, *An Autobiography,* II (London, 1934), pp. 630–1.

10 B. Webb, *Diaries 1924–1932* (London, 1956), p. 11.

11 *Parliamentary Debates*, 26 February 1924, vol. 170, paras 335–50.

12 CAB 23/47. Appendix to Conclusions of Cabinet, 11(24), 5 February 1924.

13 N. Branson, *Poplarism 1919–1925* (London, 1979), p. 215.

14 G. Lansbury, *My Life* (London, 1928), p. 167. See also R. L. Lyman, *The First Labour Government 1924* (London, 1957), pp. 133–4.

15 CAB 24/165 p. 2, para. 2, 19 February 1924.

16 *Ibid.*

17 *Ibid.*

18 I. MacLean, *The Legend of Red Clydeside* (Edinburgh. 1983), p. 218.

19 PRO 30/69, p. 211, Wheatley to MacDonald, March 1924.

20 *Parliamentary Debates*, vol. 175, para. 2,715.

21 Webb, *op. cit.*, p. 19.

22 *Ibid.*

23 T. Jones, *Whitehall Diary – 1916–25* (London, 1969), pp. 269–70.

24 *Parliamentary Debates*, 26 March 1924, vol. 171, paras 1,466–7.

25 *Ibid.*, paras 1,469–70.

26 HLG 29/130 vol. 12, 20 May 1924.

27 *Parliamentary Debates,* 3 June 1924, vol. 174, para. 1,138.

28 L. Masterman, *C. F. G. Masterman* (London, 1939), p. 348.

29 *Parliamentary Debates,* 25 July 1924, vol. 176, paras 1,726–77.

30 *Ibid.*, paras 1,703–4.

31 Masterman, *op. cit.*, p. 341.

32 Scanlon, *The Decline and Fall of the Labour Party*, p. 152.

33 E. D. Simon, *The Anti-Slum Campaign* (London, 1933), p. 25.

34 *Ibid.*, p. 23.

35 E. D. Simon, *How to Abolish the Slums* (London, 1929), p. 67.

36 M. Cowling, *The Impact of Labour* (London, 1971), p. 376. For what is still a balanced view of Wheatley's housing legislation, see Lyman, *op. cit.*, pp. 110–29.

37 *Parliamentary Debates,* 16 December 1924, vol. 179, para. 842.

38 Simon, *The Anti-Slum Campaign*, p. 35.

39 *The Times*, 13 May 1924.

40 *Ibid.*, 10 May 1924.

41 *Ibid.*

42 D. Russell, *The Tamarisk Tree* (London, 1977), p. 174.

43 *The Times*, 1 July 1924.

44 *Ibid.*, 12 August 1924.

45 *Ibid.*

46 *New Leader*, 7 November 1924.

47 *Ibid.*, 12 December 1924.

48 MacLean, *The Legend of Red Clydeside*, p. 209.

49 W. Gallacher, *Last Memoirs* (London, 1966) p. 200.

50 C. Andrew, *Secret Service – The Making of the British Intelligence Community* (London, 1985), p. 301.

Chapter 8

1 *Glasgow Herald*, 22 October 1924.

2 *New Leader*, 23 October 1924.

3 *Glasgow Herald*, 20 October 1924.

4 *Glasgow Eastern Standard*, 8 November 1924.

5 *Glasgow Observer*, 11 October 1924.

6 *Ibid.*, 10 October 1925.

7 *Ibid.*, 3 January 1925.

8 ILP Annual Conference Report, 1925, pp. 132–3. See also *New Leader*, 17 April 1925.

9 O. Mosley, *My Life* (London, 1968), p. 174.

10 *Parliamentary Debates*, 7 April 1925.

11 R. Skidelsky, *Politicians and the Slump* (London, 1967), pp. 64–5.

12 Report of the Thirty-Fourth Annual Conference of the ILP, 1926, pp. 80–6.

13 *Glasgow Evening Standard*, 22 May 1926.

14 *Ibid.*, 30 October 1926.

15 *Ibid.*

16 F. M. Leventhal, *The Last Dissenter: H. N. Brailsford and His World* (Oxford, 1985), p. 197.

17 D. Marquand, *Ramsay MacDonald* (London, 1978), p. 455.

18 J. Paton, *Left Turn* (London, 1936), p. 335.

19 *New Leader*, 24 December 1926 (later published as *Socialize the National Income!* [London, 1927]).

20 *Ibid.*

21 L. Trotsky, *Where is Britain Going?* (London, 1926).

22 *New Statesman*, 10 April 1926.

23 *Forward*, 16 July 1927.

24 *Ibid.*

25 *Ibid.*

26 A. Dewar Gibb, *Scotland in Eclipse* (London, 1930), pp. 54–5.

27 Quoted in R. K. Middlemas, *The Clydesiders* (London, 1965), p. 212.

28 *New Leader*, 14 October 1927.

29 *Forward*, 30 June 1928.

30 A. F. Brockway, *Inside the Left* (London, 1942), pp. 194–5.

31 W. Gallacher, *Last Memoirs* (London, 1966), pp. 222–5.

32 Paton, *op. cit.*, p. 301.
33 *Daily Herald*, 4 October 1928.
34 *Ibid.*
35 *Glasgow Evening Standard*, 20 October 1928.
36 *Ibid.*, 19 January 1929.
37 *Ibid.*, 9 March 1929.
38 *Ibid.*, 11 May 1929.
39 P. Snowden, *An Autobiography*, II (London, 1934), pp. 759–60.
40 Brockway, *op. cit.*, pp. 197–8. Also, conversation with the author, 26 March 1984.
41 R. E. Dowse, *Left in the Centre* (London, 1966), p. 153. See also *New Leader*, 5 July 1929.
42 Brockway, *op. cit.*, pp. 208–9.
43 *Glasgow Observer*, 29 December 1929. See also R. K. Middlemas, *The Clydesiders* (London, 1965), pp. 238–9.
44 *New Leader*, 17 January 1930.
45 *Ibid.*
46 B. Webb, *Diaries 1924–32* (London, 1956), p. 235.
47 *Ibid.*
48 *Ibid.*
49 *Ibid.*
50 *Daily Herald*, 28 April 1930.
51 *Ibid.*
52 *New Statesman*, 17 May 1930.
53 J. Scanlon, *Cast Off All Fooling* (London, 1938), p. 191.

Chapter 9

1 T. Gallagher, *Glasgow: The Uneasy Peace: Religious Tensions in Modern Scotland 1819–1914* (Manchester, 1987), especially chapters 4 and 5.
2 *Glasgow Eastern Standard*, 11 May 1929.
3 R. K. Middlemas, *The Clydesiders* (London, 1965), p. 242.
4 Lord Brockway in conversation with the author, 26 March 1984.

Sources

Primary

Over twenty years ago, in *The Clydesiders*, R. K. Middlemas referred in his bibliography to the 'Wheatley papers', but, in reality, these add up to little more than a few letters and published leaflets. The absence of any comprehensive papers sets limits to the scope of any biography, but the following collections have been drawn upon in the preparation of this study:

Ramsay MacDonald, papers, Public Record Office, Kew.
R. E. Muirhead, papers, National Library of Scotland, Edinburgh.
Emrys Hughes, papers, National Library of Scotland, Edinburgh.
James Maxton, papers, Strathclyde Regional Archive, Glasgow.
J. Walton Newbold, papers, John Rylands Library, Manchester.
P. J. Dollan, autobiographical manuscript, Baillieston Public Library, Glasgow.
Helen Crawford, autobiographical manuscript, Marx Memorial Library, London.

Manuscript and printed materials
Independent Labour Party Conference Reports, 1922–30.
Minutes of National Administrative Council of the Independent Labour Party, 1922–30.
Minutes of the Parliamentary Group of the Independent Labour Party, 1922–30.
Glasgow Independent Labour Party Federation Minutes, 1918–30.
Scottish Trades Union Congress Reports.
Glasgow Trades Council Minutes.
Scottish Council of the Labour Party Conference Reports, 1922–30.
Labour Party Report of a special committee appointed by the Annual Conference of the Party held at Manchester in 1917 to inquire into and report upon the circumstances which resulted in the Deportation in March 1916 of David Kirkwood and other workmen employed in the Munitions Factories in the Clyde District.
Shettleston Independent Labour Party Minutes, 1907–30.
Clyde Workers Defence Committee: miscellaneous papers and correspondence.

Sources

Royal Commission on the Housing of the Industrial Population of Scotland, Rural and Urban, 1917.
Court of Session Papers on 1927 action by John Wheatley against Alexander B. Anderson and J. M. Reid Miller.
Parliamentary Debates, 1922–30.
Bruce Murray News Cutting Book Collection, Strathclyde Regional Archives.

Newspapers and journals
The *Daily Herald*
Forward
The *Glasgow Eastern Standard*
The *Glasgow Evening Citizen*
The *Glasgow Evening Times*
The *Glasgow Herald*
The *Glasgow Observer*
The *Labour Magazine*
The *Mercat Cross*
The *Municipal Review*
The *Nation*
The *New Leader*
New Statesman
The *Observer*
The *Scotsman*
The *Times*

Secondary

While this book was being completed, John Hannan's *A Life of John Wheatley* (1988) was published, but, while it is the first biography of him, it is a disappointing and superficial work. Michael Fry's *Patronage and Principle: A Political History of Modern Scotland* (1987) appeared too late for much consideration, but is a stimulating treatment of its period, with a good deal on Wheatley's role. Also appearing in 1987, Tom Gallagher's *Glasgow: The Uneasy Peace: Religious Tension in Modern Scotland* has much of great value to say on the assimilation of the immigrant Irish within the organisations of the labour movement. Easily the best extended analysis of the forces which shaped Wheatley, particularly in his thinking on national questions, is David Howell's *A Lost Left* (1986). Ian McLean's *The Legend of Red Clydeside* (1983) is a very consciously revisionist view of events which were formative in Wheatley's political development, and he does not wholly succeed in his attempt to minimise Wheatley's achievements in office in 1924. *The Clydesiders* by R. K. Middlemas, published a quarter of a century ago in 1965, though flawed in parts of its approach as well as being inaccurate at times, is still a readable introduction to the period, and does show a clear grasp of Wheatley's importance. There are also memoirs which give us vivid glimpses of Wheatley and some assessment of him as a man and a socialist politician. The best of these is the second volume of John Paton's autobiography, much in need of reprinting, *Left Turn* (1936)) but also well worth consulting are Willie Gallacher's *Revolt on the Clyde* (1936) and *Last Memoirs* (1966), and Fenner Brockway's *Inside the Left* (1942).

Books and pamphlets appearing during Wheatley's lifetime
Bolitho, W., *Cancer of the Empire* (London, 1924).
Bracher, S. V., *The Herald Book of Labour Members* (London, 1923).
Cole, G. D. H., *Labour in Wartime* (Glasgow, 1915).
Denvir, J., *The Irish in Britain* (London, 1892).
Dewar Gibb, A., *Scotland in Eclipse* (London, 1930).
Haden Guest, L., *Labour and the Empire* (London, 1926).
Hamilton, M. A., *Fit to Govern* (London, 1924).
Lansbury, G., *My Life* (London, 1928).
Smart, W., *The Housing Problem and the Municipality of Glasgow* (Glasgow, 1902).
Smillie, R., *My Life for Labour* (London, 1924).
Tracey, H., *The Book of the Labour Party*, 3 vols (London, 1925).
Trotsky, L., *Where is Britain Going?* (London, 1926).
Wertheimer, E., *Portrait of the Labour Party* (London, 1929).
Wheatley, J., *How the Miners are Robbed: The Duke in the Dock* (Glasgow, 1907).
———, *The Catholic Working Man* (Glasgow, 1909).
———, *Mines, Miners and Misery* (Glasgow, 1909).
———, 'The Catholic socialist movement in Britain', *Socialist Review*, 9 April 1912, pp. 138–44.
———, *A Christian in Difficulties* (Glasgow, 1912).
———, *Eight-pound Cottages for Glasgow Citizens* (Glasgow, 1913).
———, *A Reply to the Critics of Eight-Pound Cottages* (Glasgow, 1913).
———, *Municipal Banking: How the City of Glasgow Could Save Millions* (Glasgow, 1920).
———, *The New Rent Act: A Reply to the Rent Raisers* (Glasgow, 1920).
———, *Starving in the Midst of Plenty* (Glasgow, 1923).
———, *Homes or Hutches?* (Glasgow, 1923).
———, *Labour Solves the Housing Problem: An Exposition of the Wheatley Scheme* (Glasgow, 1924).
———, *Socialize the National Income!* (Glasgow, 1927).

Sources

Later works

Abrams, P., 'The failure of social reform, 1918–20', *Past and Present*, 24 (1963), pp. 43–64.

Andrew, C., *Secret Service: The Making of the British Intelligence Community* (London, 1985).

Aspinall, B., 'The formation of the Catholic community in the west of Scotland: some preliminary outlines', *Innes Review*, 33 (1982), pp. 44–57.

Bell, T., *Pioneering Days* (London, 1941).

Bleiman, D. and Keating, M., *Labour and Scottish Nationalism* (London, 1979).

Bowley, M., *Housing and the State, 1919–44* (London, 1945).

Branson, N., *Poplarism, 1919–1925* (London, 1979).

Brockway, A. F., *Inside the Left* (London, 1942).

——, *Towards Tomorrow* (London, 1977).

Broom, J., *John MacLean* (Loanhead, 1973).

Brotherstone, T., 'The Suppression of the "Forward"', *Scottish Labour History Society Journal*, 1 (1969), pp. 5–23.

Brown, G., *Maxton* (Edinburgh, 1986).

Brown, K. D., *The First Labour Party 1906–14* (London, 1985).

Butt, J, 'Working Class Housing in Glasgow, 1900–39', in I. MacDougall (ed.), *Essays in Scottish Labour History* (Edinburgh, 1978).

Challinor, R., *The Origins of British Bolshevism* (London, 1977).

Checkland, S. G., *The Upas Tree: Glasgow, 1875–1975* (Glasgow, 1976).

Chapman, S. D. (ed.), *A History of Working-Class Housing* (Newton Abbot, 1971).

Clarke, P. F., *Liberals and Social Democrats* (Cambridge, 1979).

Clynes, J. R., *Memoirs*, 2 vols (London, 1937).

Cowling, M., *The Impact of Labour 1920–24* (London, 1971).

Cramond, R. D., *Housing Policy in Scotland 1919–64: A Study in State Assistance* (Glasgow, 1966).

Damer, S., *Rent Strike! – The Clydebank Rent Struggles of the 1920s* (Clydebank, 1982).

Dilks, D., *Neville Chamberlain 1869–1929*, I (London, 1984).

Dowse, R. E., *Left in the Centre: The Independent Labour Party 1893–1940* (London, 1966).

Englander, D., *Landlord and Tenant in Urban Britain 1838–1918* (Oxford, 1983).

—— 'Landlord and tenant in urban Scotland', *Scottish Labour History Society Journal*, 15 (1981), pp. 4–14.

Foot, M., *Aneurin Bevan* (London, 1962).

Gallacher, W., *Revolt on the Clyde* (London, 1936).

——, *Last Memoirs* (London, 1966).

Gallagher, T., *Glasgow: The Uneasy Peace: Religious Tensions in Modern Scotland 1819–1914* (Manchester, 1987).

210

——, 'Scottish Catholics and the British Left 1918–34' *Innes Review*, 34 (1983), pp. 17–42.

——, 'Red Clyde's double anniversary', *Scottish Labour History Society Journal*, 20 (1985), pp. 4–14.

Gilley, S., 'Catholics and Socialists in Glasgow 1906–12', in L. Lunn (ed.), *Immigrants and Minorities: Historical Responses to Newcomers in British Society* (London, 1980).

Graham, T. N., *Willie Graham* (London, 1948).

Haddow, A., *My Seventy Years* (Glasgow, 1943).

Hannan, J., *The Life of John Wheatley* (Nottingham, 1988).

Harvie, C., *No Gods and Precious Few Heroes: Scotland 1914–1980* (London, 1981).

Hinton, J., *The First Shop Stewards Movement* (London, 1973).

——, 'The suppression of the *"Forward"* – a note', *Scottish Labour History Society Journal*, 7 (1973), pp. 4–9.

Hobson, J. T. A., *The Economics of Unemployment* (London, 1922).

Howell, D., *British Workers and the Independent Labour Party 1888–1906* (Manchester, 1983).

——, *A Lost Left – Three Studies in Socialism and Nationalism* (Manchester, 1986).

Jackson, S., *My Ain Folk* (Glasgow, 1981).

Johnston, T., *Memories* (London, 1952).

Jones, T., *Whitehall Diary – 1916–25* (London, 1969).

Keynes, J. M., *Tract for Monetary Reform* (London, 1923).

Kirkwood, D., *My Life of Revolt* (London, 1935).

Knox, W. (ed.), *Scottish Labour Leaders 1918–39* (Edinburgh, 1984).

Lee, J., *Tomorrow is a New Day* (London, 1939).

——, *My Life With Nye* (London, 1980).

Leventhal, F. M., *The Last Dissenter: H. N. Brailsford and his World* (Oxford, 1985).

Lyman, R., *The First Labour Government 1924* (London, 1957).

McAllister, G., *James Maxton: Portrait of a Rebel* (London, 1935).

McCaffrey J., 'The Irish vote in Glasgow in the later nineteenth century', *Innes Review*, 31 (1970), pp. 30–6.

MacDougall, I. (ed.), *Essays in Scottish Labour History* (Edinburgh, 1978).

——, *Labour Records in Scotland* (Edinburgh, 1978).

McGovern, J., *Without Fear or Favour* (Edinburgh, 1978).

McHugh, J., 'The Clyde rent strike 1915', *Scottish Labour History Society Journal*, 12 (1978), pp. 56–63.

MacKenzie, C., *Catholicism in Scotland* (London, 1936).

McKibben, R. *The Evolution of the Labour Party 1910–24* (Oxford, 1974).

MacLean, I., *The Legend of Red Clydeside* (Edinburgh, 1983).

MacLean, I., 'Red Clydeside 1915-19', in R. Quinault and J. Stevenson (eds), *Popular Protest and Public Order* (London, 1974).

——, 'The Ministry of Munitions, the Clyde Workers Committee and the suppression of the *"Forward"*: an alternative view', *Scottish Labour History Society Journal*, 6 (1972), pp. 3–25.

McNair, J., *James Maxton, the Beloved Rebel* (London, 1955).

McShane, H. and Smith, J., *Harry McShane: No Mean Fighter* (London, 1978).

McWhirter, J., 'Internationalism and the British labour movement 1917–27', *Scottish Labour History Society Journal*, 6 (1972) pp. 26–54.

Middlemas, R. K., *The Clydesiders: A Left-Wing Struggle for Parliamentary Power* (London, 1965).

Mosley, O., *My Life* (London, 1968).

Muir, E., *Autobiography* (London, 1954).

Nicolson, H., *King George V: His Life and Reign* (London, 1952).

Oakley, C. A., *The Second City* (London and Glasgow, 1946).

O'Brien, C. C., *Parnell and his Party* (Oxford, 1957).

Page Arnot, R., *The Scottish Miners* (London, 1955).

Paton, J., *Left Turn* (London, 1936).

Reader, W. J., *Architect of Air Power* (London, 1968).

Russell, D., *The Tamarisk Tree* (London, 1977).

Scanlon, J., *The Decline and Fall of the Labour Party* (London, 1932).

——, *Cast Off All Fooling* (London, 1938).

Shinwell, E., *Conflict Without Malice* (London, 1955).

——, *I've Lived through it all* (London, 1973).

Simon, E. D., *How to Abolish the Slums* (London, 1929).

——, *The Anti-Slum Campaign* (London, 1933).

Skidelsky, R., *Politicians and the Slump* (London, 1967).

——, *Oswald Mosley* (London, 1975).

Snowden, P., *An Autobiography* (London, 1934).

Vidler, A., *A Century of Social Catholicism* (London, 1964)

Walker, W. 'Irish immigrants in Scotland: their priests, politics and parochial life', *Historical Journal* (1972), pp. 649–67.

Webb, B., *Diaries 1924–32* (London, 1956).

Winter, J. M., *Socialism and the Challenge of War: Ideas and Politics in Britain 1912-18* (London, 1974).

Wood, I. S., 'Irish Immigrants and Scottish Radicalism 1880–1906', in I. MacDougall (ed.), *Essays in Scottish Labour History* (Edinburgh, 1978).

——, 'John Wheatley, the Irish and the labour movement in Scotland', *Innes Review*, 31 (1980), pp. 71–87.

Wrigley, C. J., *Lloyd George and the British Labour Movement* (Sussex, 1976).

Young, J. D., *The Rousing of the Scottish Working Class* (London, 1979).

Theses, dissertations

Cooper, S., 'John Wheatley: A Study in Labour History', Ph.D. thesis, University of Glasgow, 1973.

Brown, G., 'The Labour Party and Political Change in Scotland (1918–1929): The Politics of Five Elections', Ph.D. thesis, Edinburgh, 1982.

Gunnin, G. C., 'John Wheatley, Catholic Socialism and Irish Labour in the West of Scotland', Ph.D. thesis, University of Chicago, 1973.

Purdie, R., 'Outside the Chapel Door – the Glasgow Catholic Socialist Society 1906–1922', unpublished dissertation, University of Oxford, 1976.

Kane, P. 'Catholic Socialist – A Brief Account of the Life and Times of John Wheatley', unpublished manuscript in the Mitchell Library, Glasgow. 1970.

Earley, M. 'John Wheatley and Left-Wing Socialism', M.Sc. dissertation, University of London, 1977.

Index

214